# Cogswell & Harrison

## Two Centuries of Gunmaking

# COGSWELL & HARRISON

## TWO CENTURIES *of* GUNMAKING

GRAHAM COOLEY &
JOHN NEWTON

· THE ·
SPORTSMAN'S
PRESS
*LONDON*

Published by The Sportsman's Press 2000

DEDICATIONS

*To all those unselfconscious artist craftsmen,*
*usually unnamed and unrecognised,*
*whose expertise has bequeathed*
*the elegance and brilliant functionality*
*that characterises a fine sporting gun.*

*To Anne and Charles*

NOTE
Most of the prices quoted in the text are pre decimal coinage. As a reminder, there were 12 pennies (d) in a shilling (s or /-), and 20 shillings to a pound (£). A guinea was 21s (21/-). A price in shillings was often quoted as, say 12/6 (i.e. 12 shillings and 6 pence). A shilling is equivalent to 5 pence today.

All the Patent Numbers quoted in this book are British, except where indicated.

A catalogue record for this book
is available from the British Library

ISBN 0-948-253-83-5

Printed in Great Britain by
BAS Printers Ltd, Over Wallop, Hampshire

Although at present the English Sporting Gun trade enjoys an amazing supremacy, it must not rest content with the laurels gained. Competitors are active, and we must look forward. Instruction to youths in the trade is a necessity and technical training must be looked to, for if we once lose the lead it might never be regained.

*Edgar Harrison, chairing the 5th Annual Dinner of the Gunmakers' Association at the Trocadero Restaurant, London, 9 May 1900*

*Motto: I neither despise nor fear*

The Cogswell Coat of Arms copied for Benjamin Cogswell in 1882 by the Heralds Office and used for his business. It was originally granted in 1337 to Sir John de Coggeshall by Edward III. Several spellings of this name are recognised by the College of Heralds.

Edgar Harrison (1858 - 1938)
Chairman of Cogswell & Harrison 1896 - 1938
Chairman of the Gunmakers' Association 1901 and 1912
Master of the Gunmakers' Company 1924

# Contents

# List of Colour Plates

Plate 10   A matched pair of Victor sidelock ejectors also shown on the front cover, Nos 44,979/44,980, built in 1912. *(Courtesy J. Baert.)*

Plate 11   A matched pair of 12-bore Extra Quality Victor SLEs, Nos. 47,421/2, completed in 1920. *(Courtesy A. Brierley.)*

Plate 12   A 12-bore boxlock fitted with Southgate ejectors, No. 55,181. It was sold from the Exeter shop on 18 December 1925. *(J. Newton collection.)*

Cogswell & Harrison gun cases.

Plate 13   A section of the Cogswell & Harrison 20-volume company archive. Details of most C&H guns are recorded in great detail. *(Bookcase by Charles Wickham).*

A Cogswell & Harrison sidelock ejector over-and-under, No. 57,434. Work commenced on 24 September 1937 but was suspended for the duration of World War Two. The gun was not completed and sold until 18 June 1947. *(Courtesy J. Congram.)*

Plate 14   A 12-bore Regency, one of the 'Guns of Distinction' introduced in 1970 to commemorate the company bicentenary. This model is still available in all calibres.

Plate 15   The locks of a new Cogswell & Harrison Best London self-opening SLE.

Plate 16   An Extra Quality Victoria (special) 20-bore BLE with round body, chopperlump barrels, intercepting sears and removable crosspin. These are current and may be ordered in all calibres. *(Courtesy A.J. Bird.)*

*Photos: Ann Bolton, Plates 9 (below) and 12; David Clare, Plate 13 (below); David Grant, Plates 1, 3, 4, 7 (top), 8 (top), 9 (top), 10, 11, 13 (top), 14, 15, 16.*

# Authors' Foreword and Acknowledgements

This book charts the history of Cogswell & Harrison from its origins in 1770, through its bicentenary in 1970 and up to its restructuring in 1993.

That time span marks the company out as London's oldest surviving gunmaker. Given the pre-eminence of London gunmaking that is an enviable plaudit. However, it is not without its problems for those attempting to excavate its early history. It is generally true that the further back in history one goes the less clear are the marks in the sands of time. Whilst Cogswell & Harrison's history is comparatively well documented over the last 100 years, the first 130 proved to be far more problematic.

During long periods there is little original source material apart from a few tantalising snippets, so there are gaps in the early history we have been unable to fill. Records were lost for a number of reasons. Two major fires, occasional floods and the changes in company premises would have consumed some of them, as would the often haphazard book- and record-keeping. In other cases, paperwork was no doubt discarded by those who did not realise its significance in historical terms.

This work has therefore drawn very heavily on *Bicentenary of a Gunmaker* published by Cogswell & Harrison in 1970 and based on John Peskett's lifetime notes during his 60 years' service with the company. Without Peskett's little 44 page book, much of the story would be irretrievably lost. Even his notes cannot be located and may also have been discarded, so his witness to the events described provide the basis on which we have built much of the story.

Thus piecing together the early history of the company has proved to be quite difficult. From the onset we hoped to locate ever more relevant material, the eternal wish of the historical researcher and we freely admit that in the chapters that follow, some gaps and slight inconsistencies may be detected in the early years of Cogswell & Harrison.

As to the period from 1850 to the present day, we were most fortunate in having the close collaboration of the present owners of the company. They facilitated access to the company's extensive archive including 20 huge volumes of gun and product records, a collection of original books, catalogues, letter and manufacturing information and procedures. They were ever helpful in advising on the interpretation of the records and contributed significantly in assisting us with a wealth of information to supplement our own research.

From a technical point of view, a survey of all the patent applications and in particular those by Edgar Harrison, provided a particularly vivid insight into the ingenuity and creativity of the London gun trade.

In addition to the general historical sections, we have provided a series of appendices which we trust will be of use to researchers, collectors and owners of Cogswell & Harrison guns.

We are indebted to: Mike Cooley, Alan Crewe and Shirley Pullen of Cogswell & Harrison Ltd for the wealth of information provided and their continued support over the years this book was being researched and written and to David Grant for photography; Kenneth Kemp of The Sportsman's Press who initiated the project at the Game Fair some years ago and who has advised and supported us throughout the project; the *Shooting Times* and the *Shooting Gazette* who notified their readers that we were keen to locate unusual company products and memorabilia and their many readers who responded so helpfully; the auction houses were generous in allowing us to use illustrations from their catalogues and we thank Angus Barnes of Bonhams, Chris Austyn of Christies, Adrian Weller of Sothebys and Nicholas Holt of Holt & Co. We are also indebted to Alan Print for invaluable assistance with patent searching.

Many individuals provided us with background material or sent us old catalogues and documents. We would like to mention in particular: Judge Baker QC, Roger Baxandall, Jeff Bird, Ann Bolton, Geoffrey Boothroyd, Rupert Chenevix-Trench, David Clark, Mr A. Cleave, Jackie Cogswell, John Congram, Chris

Craddock, Ann Crewe, Ian Crudgington, J.C. Divine Inc., Lewis Drake, Michael Evans, Lt Gen. K.E. Fletcher, Don Gustine, Mr C. Hallatt, Bill Harriman, James M. Kilday, Dr Killidar, Julian Murray-Evans, Charles Murray-Roscoe, Anne Newton, Emil Rosner, Brent Johnson, Roger G. Sanger, Christopher Scott, Roger Slater, Rod Sykes, Don and Janet Simmons, Douglas Tate, Andrew Tucker, Alison Walder, Sam Wells, Charles Wickham, Emma Wilson.

Our special thanks are extended to Sue Coley who did the final editing. Her patience and perserverance in the face of continual changes and delayed material was exemplary.

We hope you enjoy the story.

*Graham Cooley and John Newton*
*August 2000*

# Introduction

The history of Cogswell & Harrison makes a fascinating story. In some form or another it has spanned four centuries. It is also one of the very few gunmaking companies which, at the beginning of the twenty-first century, is still family owned.

The story begins in 1770 at the heart of London gunmaking, proceeds through the extraordinary innovations of Edgar Harrison and ends, 230 years later, with business diversification, voluntary liquidation, guardianship and eventual rebirth. Its convoluted history, its triumphs and tribulations and the challenges it faces in the new century can only be properly understood in the context of the London gun trade as a whole.

Since the eighteenth century, London gunmakers have produced some of the finest sporting guns in the world. It is now often pointed out that the London gun trade is but a shadow of its former self. While no doubt correct in terms of quantity, it is certainly incorrect in terms of quality. It is a fact that the number of London gunmakers has dwindled over the years. It is also a fact that the work of London craftsmen still sets the standard by which quality guns are judged worldwide.

The story of the London gun trade and its rise to pre-eminence in the nineteenth century starts with the extraordinary Manton brothers, John and Joseph. John was born in 1752 and following a gunmaking apprenticeship in Leicester and Grantham, he moved to London in 1781 to set up in his own right at 6 Dover Street, Piccadilly. His younger brother, Joseph Manton, was born in 1766 and from 1781 he completed his apprenticeship with his famous older brother.

From the onset the brothers displayed great technical innovation and an almost ruthless insistence on the very best workmanship. Indeed, they epitomized what modern management theorists refer to as 'a culture of continuous improvement and innovation'. They perfected the flintlock mechanism and set gunmaking standards which gradually became the benchmark of other London makers. By the end of the eighteenth century the quality of work in the London gun trade surpassed that of the excellent gunmakers in France, Germany, Belgium and Italy.

The beginning of the nineteenth century saw the emergence of gunmakers such as Joseph Lang, Charles Lancaster, George Daw and others. This was the context in which Cogswell & Harrison developed. The ferment of creativity and inventiveness of the period that followed was reflected in Cogswell & Harrison by the Ingenious Harrisons, Edward and Edgar from 1864 to 1929. By the end of the nineteenth century the famous gunmaking companies were in the main to be found in the Strand area, Piccadilly and Mayfair and Cogswell & Harrison was no exception, having addresses in the Strand, New Bond Street and Piccadilly.

The London gun trade, in common with other industries, experienced problems of inflation and depression in the 1930s. However, over and above many other sectors of industry, it suffered the loss of the traditional markets due to the break up of the British Empire. All of this was further exacerbated in the post-war years by the influx of foreign guns, some admittedly good quality and value for money. In addition, the growth of clay pigeon shooting with less expensive, machine-made guns meant a contraction of the market for handmade London guns.

The last 25 years has seen something of a renaissance for the London gun trade with the re-emergence of such names as Beesley, Churchill, Atkin, Grant & Lang, Watson and Hellis. In 1993 Cogswell & Harrison was restructured under the new management of Mike Cooley and Alan Crewe.

This is the backdrop against which this present book was written. As with any book it reflects at least in part, the particular concerns and interests of its authors. In this context it concentrates on the company's gunmaking activities and refers only in passing to the company's several diversification projects including the manufacture and sale of wider sporting goods.

It is hoped that by providing a history of Cogswell & Harrison this book will be a useful contribution to the history of the London gun trade. It is also intended as a tribute to the craftsmen whose skill and dedication have given so much to those who enjoy fine English guns which are now assets to be passed from one generation to another.

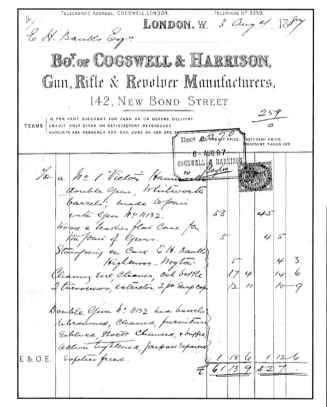

# Significant Dates

1770   Benjamin Cogswell goes into business at 4 Bengal Place, New Kent Road, London.

1794   Hector Essex (said to be a relation of Cogswell), hardware man at 224 Strand, London.

1805   Hector Essex, gunsmith and jeweller at 104 and 223/224 Strand.

1821   Robert Essex, brother of Hector, Silversmith and dealer in firearms. Succeeds to business at 224 Strand.

1835   Edward Benton, silversmith and firearms dealer, takes over 224 Strand.

1842   Between 1830 and 1842 Benjamin Cogswell was described as a pawnbroker at 4 Bengal Place. Benjamin Cogswell takes over the 224 Strand address. Advertises himself as 'Gun and Pistol Warehouse' (successor to Edward Benton).

1857   Advertises himself as Benjamin Cogswell gunmaker at 224 Strand.

1863   Benjamin Cogswell (Jnr) takes Edward Harrison into partnership.
B. Cogswell becomes Cogswell & Harrison at 224 Strand.

1879   Strand premises run in conjunction with new business managed by Edgar Harrison at 142 New Bond Street, London.

1882   Firm becomes a Limited Company. Moves to 226 Strand.

1886   Edward Harrison leases factory at Ferndale Estate in Harrow, Middlesex. Edgar Harrison and Julia Adlas Chaplin owners of Cogswell & Harrison and E. Harrison & Co.

1887   Edgar Harrison takes new lease on Harrow factory. Edgar Harrison and Julia Chaplin enter new business partnership. Edgar Harrison resides at Hindes Road, Harrow.

1891   Armourers Club founded (forerunner of the Gun Trade Association). E. Harrison founder member.

1893   Premises leased at 29a Gillingham Street, Victoria, London. Sidney Harrison said to have been based there.

1901   Edgar Harrison is Chairman of the Gunmakers' Association (predecessor to the Gun Trade Association).

1908   Cogswell and Harrison acquire William Moore and Grey of Craven Street, Strand.

1912   Edgar Harrison is Chairman of the Gunmakers' Association.

1915   Cogswell Harrison, the only son of Edgar Harrison, is killed in explosion at the company's powder mills and shooting grounds in Colnbrook.

1917   New West End premises open at 168 Piccadilly, London.

1919   Claude Harrison joins H.H. Hussey to form Harrison & Hussey at 41 Albemarle  Street, London.

1924   Edgar Harrison is Master of the Worshipful Company of Gunmakers.

1930   Harrison & Hussey (independent company) closes.

1932   Voluntary liquidation is followed by the formation of Cogswell and Harrison (1932) Ltd.

1938   Edgar Harrison dies. His son-in-law, Major Cordova, becomes Chairman with John Peskett as Managing Director.

1957   Sam Cummings, President of International Armaments Corp. of the US and Canada, becomes majority shareholder.

1958   Sam Cummings acquires several well-known London Gunmakers including Churchill, Boswell and Cogswell & Harrison to form InterArm Co., which also included Cogswell & Harrison.

1963   Existing directors, including John Peskett and Ted Holden purchase back Cogswell & Harrison from InterArm Co.

1970   Bicentenary celebrations.

1982   Extraordinary general meeting on 26 April resolves that the company goes into voluntary liquidation. Maurice Sidney Chaplan appointed liquidator.

1983   Farlows of Pall Mall acquire the name and goodwill of Cogswell & Harrison.

1984   Farlows issues gunmaking license to J. Roberts & Son. Continues for five years.

1993   Cooley family purchases Cogswell & Harrison together with all rights.

1993   Mike Cooley and Alan Crewe relaunch the company.

# Part One: Company History

This Benjamin Cogswell pistol was built to his Registered Design No. 3,389 of 16 November 1852.

# 1 The Origins of the Company

The name of Cogswell was found on numerous weapons in the
possession of army officers, duellists, coastguards, buccaneers
and even highwaymen.

John Peskett, *Bicententary of a Gunmaker*

## Benjamin Cogswell Senior

When Benjamin Cogswell established a business in May 1770, he could not
have imagined that even past the millennium, shooting sportsmen worldwide
would be familiar with his name and the company that later emerged from it.
Neither would he have foreseen the eventual production of thousands of weapons
bearing the name Cogswell together with that of his son's later business partner,
Edward Harrison. It was from his modest workshop at 4 Bengal Place, New Kent
Road, London during the reign of George III that Benjamin Cogswell laid the basis
for London's oldest surviving gunmaking business which later became the company Cogswell & Harrison Limited.

It is not clear what Benjamin Cogswell called his business but he took advantage
of the huge demand for firearms created by the Napoleonic wars to set up facilities
for turning out hand-made pistols in an expanding market. Tragically, many a young
soldier came to an abrupt end from a Cogswell firearm and highwaymen occasion-
ally had possession of them. Cogswell was an astute businessman employing only
the best craftsmen. With a high reputation for his own capabilities, the skill of his
employees and the standard of his products, Cogswell retained a firm hold on this
market. There were few reliable gunmakers at the time and the best ones were very
highly regarded.

After Waterloo, the officers and other gentlemen now home from war were developing into keen sportsmen and Cogswell satisfied their demand for flint-lock fowling
pieces and percussion muzzle-loading guns both single- and double-barrelled. His

Benjamin Cogswell

business supplied samples 'on approval' and 'on loan' to stim-
ulate the demand for Cogswell guns – an original marketing
strategy for those days.

Duelling pistols were in demand and had to be accurate up
to twenty paces. These pistols were usually sold in perfectly
balanced and matched pairs. The weapons came with a guar-
antee that they would not hang or misfire, and that 'pull-off'
was instant so that honour could be satisfied with no mishap
due to the firearm.

In the 1820s the 'Pepper Pot' pistol was introduced. The
casting usually containing six barrels was rotated by a ratchet.
This weapon was later upgraded when the percussion cap had
superseded the flint-lock and the 'Pepper Pot' became self-
cocking.

Cogswell was later able to purchase a business in a more

Benjamin Cogswell's
trade label.

Benjamin junior's advertisement from *Sporting Magazine
Advertiser* of December 1853

prestigious area of London, from Edward Benton at 223-224 Strand London. His predecessors were the two Essex brothers who were also related to him. The trade label of this period states 'B. Cogswell Gun, Rifle & Pistol Manufacturer, 224 Strand near Temple Bar.' The business offered pawnbroking and gun storage services. Weapons were frequently pledged there to meet gambling debts.

## Benjamin Cogswell Junior

Benjamin Cogswell Junior had been admitted into the business and trained as a gun-smith by his father who continued to take a role in the administration until quite an old man. Benjamin Junior's advertisement in the *Sporting Magazine* of 1853 reads: 'B. Cogswell (late Essex), the oldest gun and pistol repository in London, established 1770, 224, Strand (near Temple Bar). Thus it appears that, although Cogswell Jnr was a gunmaker, gun dealer and gun repairer he was still referring to his business as a repository. In this advertisement, Cogswell confirms the founding date of 1770.

Despite this, the number of guns and pistols bearing the B. Cogswell name are small as compared with those bearing the Cogswell & Harrison name. This is as would be expected even though at one stage, the Cogswells had a separate related business in barrel making. The Cogswells were active over a much shorter period than were the Harrisons and much of their business was trading in a wide range of secondhand guns and pistols. Furthermore, Cogswell declared that his stock comprised every London maker of eminence, affording a most advantageous opportunity for selecting genuine secondhand guns. He went on to point out that 4-, 5-, 6- and 9-barrel self-revolving pistols were available for three guineas to 12 guineas each.

Amongst collectors, it is for their pistols that the Cogswells are remembered. Not only were these of very high quality, they frequently included innovative development. Whilst the Harrisons may be remembered for their patents in respect of shotguns, the Cogswells can be remembered for their registered designs in respect of pistols. They displayed a special interest in revolving mechanisms for these pistols. In 1848, Cogswell registered his design for a 'revolving and self-priming pistol'. This was registered as design No. 1,378 of 2 March 1848.

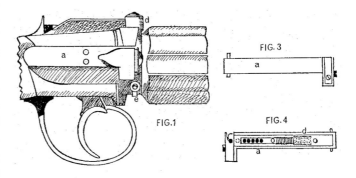

(above) Cogwell's Registered Design No. 1,378 of 2 March 1848
(below) Registered Design No. 3,389 of 16 November 1852.

Throughout that period the innovations were incorporated into their day-to-day gun-making activities. Cogswell's registered design No. 3,389 of 16 November 1852 for 'an improved six shot rifle pistol' is a case in point. It would appear that only a few of these were made and they are quite rare. Their influence on the subsequent design of revolvers will be clear from the diagram.

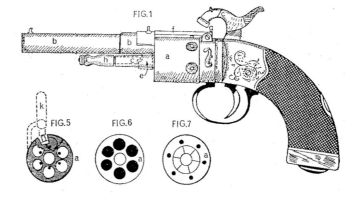

223-4 The Strand, London, in 1889.

### Edward Harrison

Cogswell & Harrison revolver No. 886, based on Webley patent, completed February 1900.
*(Photo courtesy of Honoré Mercier)*

In 1863 Benjamin Cogswell Junior took Edward Harrison into partnership. Harrison was a firearms expert, respected in the trade and a popular personality. As a consequence, the premises at 224 Strand became a place for well-known sportsmen to gather, seek advice from Harrison and exchange information with each other.

Apart from their sporting gun sales, Cogswell & Harrison made a significant profit from the supply of small arms to the French during the Franco-Prussian war. William Tranter, a famous pistol expert and close friend of Edgar Harrison collaborated with the company at this stage. Many Tranter pistols were produced bearing the Cogswell & Harrison name.

Due to the rebuilding of the Judges' entrance to the Inner Temple, 224 Strand had to be vacated and in 1883, the business (now a limited company) was moved to 226 Strand facing the Law Courts. The craftsmen worked in the basement, and the showroom, filled with racks and showcases for guns, rifles and pistols was on the ground floor. The three higher floors were used for offices and stores. When a new stairway was built, the first floor was converted into another showroom and later opened as a sports department catering for tennis players and golfers.

The Judges' entrance to the Inner Temple had cut off part of the building leaving the rooms long and narrow. Taking advantage of this, a golf practice room was established where customers could drive a softball into a net. This was the first indoor golf practice room in London and possibly in the country. Naturally it attracted competition level players and rich customers. Law Court Judges were frequent users of the practice room.

Records of Benjamin Cogswell Junior are sparse. Many of the early records were lost in a disastrous fire in 1922. Had these records survived they would no doubt have revealed further information about the Cogswells. It seems certain however, that had Cogswell Junior been still involved after the move to 226 Strand there would have been some information on this.

## Edgar Harrison

Edgar Harrison joined the business in 1874 and in 1879 he took out a lease on 141 New Bond Street. Edgar had a business partnership with a Julia Adlas Chaplin who was the lessor of 226 Strand, later to be purchased by Cogswell & Harrison. She also owned the site of the Harrow factory leased to him and at one stage they were joint owners of Cogswell & Harrison and E. Harrison & Co. Edgar and Anna, his wife, had two children: Ethel, born in 1890 and Cogswell Edgar in 1892.

When he died in 1938, Edgar Harrison had been with the company for over 50 years, and Chairman for 42 of those years. He is the most significant person in the Cogswell & Harrison story and much more detail on his accomplishments follows in later chapters.

## 2  Claude Harrison

The Bond Street premises, under the management of Claude Harrison, was lavishly decorated and carpeted as befitted a meeting place for the elite of the sporting world. Claude Harrison was always scrupulously dressed in morning clothes, and he encouraged his staff to mingle with the customers. Many a customer in those days would order a set of four shotguns or a pair with spare barrels. When opportune, Claude Harrison expected his staff to visit their homes or estates.

Part of the showroom was set aside for customers to talk among themselves or read sporting magazines laid out on a beautiful polished table on which writing materials were also available. Sportsmen exchanged shooting gossip in this section of the showroom on a daily basis and advised each other on guns and rifles according to future shooting prospects.

In 1919 Claude Harrison resigned and formed the short-lived but renowned Harrison and Hussey Ltd in partnership with H.H. Hussey. Claude Harrison was the Chairman and Managing Director, and H.H. Hussey the Gunmaker. Their company traded from its premises at 41 Albemarle St and had shooting grounds extending to 150 acres adjoining Worcester Park station, known initially as the Wimbledon Grounds and later as the Albemarle Grounds.

In 1921 Hussey left to join Ogden Smiths, he died in 1933. Harrison and Hussey continued trading until Claude Harrison died on 20 June 1929. In 1930 Stephen Grant & Joseph Lang Ltd acquired the Harrison & Hussey name and goodwill together with those of Watson Bros., Lancaster and Beesley, thus saving these names from oblivion.

W. R. H. Robson, joint managing director of Stephen Grant & Joseph Lang Ltd, is credited with the takeover of Harrison & Hussey.

An advertisement from *Game and Gun*, 1927.

# Harrison & Hussey Ltd.
## 11/10
### PER 100

ALL BRITISH · ALL BRITISH · ALL BRITISH · ALL BRITISH

THE "CURZON" SPECIAL CARTRIDGE

## 11/10
### PER 100

**12 BORE only.**  For Cash with Order.

Guaranteed Smokeless Powder and full charge of Shot.

SPECIAL CASH QUOTATION FOR ORDERS OF 5,000 UPWARDS.
Carriage Paid by Goods train on 500. Passenger train 1/- per 100.

| 16 BORE: | 20 BORE: |
|----------|----------|
| **15/-** PER 100 | **14/-** PER 100 |

MANUFACTURERS OF EJECTOR GUNS FROM 18 to 126 GUINEAS.

PLEASE ASK FOR FULL PRICE LISTS FREE.

**41, ALBEMARLE STREET, LONDON, W.1.**
Telegrams: WEAPONLESS, PICCY., LONDON.     Telephone: GERRARD 2300.
**and WORCESTER PARK, SURREY; SHOOTING GROUNDS, Worcester Park.**
Telephone: MALDEN 0257.

# 3 Wm Moore & Grey

In 1908, the well established gun dealer, Wm Moore & Grey of Craven Street, London was purchased by Cogswell & Harrison. The business had a respected place in the history of London gunmaking. It is one of the companies that provide a direct link back to Joseph Manton (1766-1835), the illustrious founder of what we now recognise as the modern London Gun Trade.

William Moore, a stocker and William Parker Grey, an administrator, both worked for Joseph Manton. However, William Moore set up in his own name at 118 Whitechapel in 1808 and in 1836 was appointed Gunmaker-in-Ordinary to William IV. Some years later, the company trade label, declared itself gun manufacturers to HRH Prince Albert and advertised 'double and single rifles upon superior principles'. It was not until a third move in 1847 to 78 Edgware Road that the business name was changed to William Moore & William Grey.

In 1854 the firm was called William Grey & Son. William Moore & Co moved to 43 Old Bond Street. From 1873 until 1902 the names were again combined in various ways with the firm's title ending up as William Moore & Grey, firstly at 165 Piccadilly and then at 8 Craven Street, Strand, also the address of Bozard & Co. It seems that the Grey in this title was Robert, William Grey's son.

The company has many claims to fame. Frederick Beesley (1846-1928) was apprenticed to William Moore in 1861 at the age of 15. He subsequently worked in the London Gun Trade and eventually at Purdey until 1879 when he set up on his own behalf in Edgware Road. Several of Beesley's inventions were also sold to Woodward and to Cogswell & Harrison. In addition, he was a joint patentee with Edward Harrison of a hammerless cocking mechanism (see page 65).

Another key figure who worked with Wm Moore and Grey was Henry Atkin. He was apprenticed to his father at Purdey – also Henry Atkin, who is said to be the first man Purdey employed. Henry Atkin the younger remained at Purdey for some ten years before joining William Moore & Grey in 1866 at 43 Old Bond Street (William Moore & Co initially). He stayed with the company for the next eleven years until setting up in his own right around 1877 at 18 Oxendon Street.

William Moore and William Grey trade label.

The company also had a branch at 11 The Arcade, Aldershot, Surrey. For some time Cogswell & Harrison had been making guns for the firm which William Moore & Grey sold with their name engraved on the action and barrels.

In 1908 Cogswell & Harrison acquired the company of Wm Moore & Grey. There is some confusion surrounding the date of acquisition, Richard Akehurst for instance gives it as 'mid 1920s'. This possibly arises because Robert Grey was working for Cogswell & Harrison in the Strand until

his death in 1928. Shortly thereafter the Craven Street lease was surrendered, and the stock and books taken over by the Strand shop. The William Moore & Grey records transferred to the Strand have never been located by Cogswell & Harrison.

As the owners of William Moore and Grey, Cogswell & Harrison marketed a gun under the name Moorgrey and these are itemised in the company's records.

In an article in the *Shooting Times*, Geoffrey Boothroyd expressed the desire to see William Moore & Grey guns again produced. This is a possibility that the directors of Cogswell & Harrison are now considering.

**William Moore & Grey Company Names and Addresses:**

| Date | Company Name | Address |
| --- | --- | --- |
| 1808 | William Moore | 118 Whitechapel |
| 1818 | William Moore | Colchester Street |
| 1828-46 | William Moore | 78 Edgware Road |
| 1847-53 | William Moore and William Grey | 78 Edgware Road |
| 1854 | William Moore & Co. | 78 Edgware Road |
| 1854 | W. Grey & Son | 78 Edgware Road |
| 1854-72 | Wm Moore & Co. | 43 Old Bond Street |
| 1873 | Wm Moore, Grey & Co | 43 Old Bond Street |
| 1874-77 | Wm Moore & Grey | 43 Old Bond Street |
| 1878-96 | Wm Moore & Grey Ltd. | 43 Old Bond Street |
| 1896 | Wm Moore & Grey | 43 Old Bond Street |
| 1896 | Wm Moore & Grey | 165 Piccadilly |
| 1902 | Wm Moore & Grey | 8 Craven Street, Strand |
| 1908 | Purchased by Cogswell & Harrison | 223 The Strand |

# 4 To Diversify or not to Diversify

To diversify or not to diversify, that is the question debated at business schools, in boardrooms and in the business press. It is also a question which engaged, some might even say haunted Cogswell & Harrison over a period of 120 years.

The early stages of the company's expansion and diversification was in what we would nowadays call its core business activities. When in 1886 Edward Harrison leased the Harrow factory, it was with a view to increasing the number and variety of weapons to be produced. The development of the Swiftsure trap in 1888 emerged from the desire to satisfy the market need for sportsmen to get out of season practice. The shooting ground facilities at Colnbrook and Malden, with their tuition and gun fitting facilities, were an extension of this business aim.

The 150 yard underground shooting range at Gillingham Street with its plating walls for testing patterns also had facilities for zeroing rifles. All this diversification came from the immediate needs of the shooting sportsman.

Diversification of another kind was taking place in Cogswell & Harrison's gunmaking which was also within its core activities. This emerged from a realisation that social and economic changes in the fabric of British life would mean that a much wider spectrum of the population could afford to shoot. However, few could pay the price of a best gun. This resulted in a range of modestly priced boxlocks using what were, at that time, radically new production methods.

## The 14³/4-Bore Gun

Those who use shotguns and the gunmakers who produce them have long sought the shotgun Holy Grail: a gun that is light, easy on the shoulder with exceptional performance and consistency in the field when in the hands of an excellent shot.

Over the years many attempts have been made to provide this ideal. Churchill would swear by his 25 in. barrels while others advocated the Lancaster 12/20 (a 12-bore of 20-bore weight). The 2 in. chambered 12-bore shooting ¹³/16 or ⁷/8 oz has many supporters to this day. In some areas of the continent, 16-bores were the preferred option.

In America at the time of writing, 20-bores with a variety of chamber lengths and chokes have their supporters and are no longer regarded as suitable only for ladies or boys as they were in the early part of the twentieth century. With modern ammunition and used with proficiency, they can frequently produce results which even committed 12-bore users find impressive. However, these preferences have much to do with personal choice and fashion.

In the early 1900s Cogswell & Harrison addressed these matters with a radical proposal. It introduced an entirely new size of breech loading gun - the 14³/4-bore. It was claimed that this new bore size was suitable for a shot charge of 1 oz or ¹/16 oz and therefore not dissimilar from the 12-bore. Furthermore, it produced patterns of equally high standards both inside and outside the 30 in. circle. It was claimed that this gun improved on a 12-bore in that it produced higher velocity, greater penetration and longer range. Over and above all of this it was on average 6 oz lighter than a comparable 12-bore.

Cogswell & Harrison produced its own 14³/4-bore cartridges using its own smokeless powder, Vicmite, which the company pointed out occupied a reduced space in the cartridge and burned without residue. Once you purchased, loyalty was assured since you had to go back to Cogswell & Harrison for the cartridges!

These 14³/4-bore guns were made in a number of grades appropriately proportioned throughout and at a cost somewhat greater than the 12-bore equivalent. For example, around 1910, the top of the range Victor grade 14³/4-bore cost 70 guineas which was 5 guineas more than the Victor best gun in 12-bore.

Very few 14³/4-bore guns or cartridges survive. The authors have spent two years attempting to find an example to photograph with no luck.

An interesting gun diversification was the 'Vena' contractor gun which was essentially a 20-bore gun but with an enlarged breech end capable of shooting 12-bore cartridges. There was the 14¾ bore gun, the walking stick air cane, through to a novel air pistol, the 'Certus'. Another diversification was into the manufacture of cartridges.

The above can be regarded as diversification within the company's core business. However, the company also entered into diversification in non-core activities.

When Cogswell & Harrison became a limited company in 1882 and moved shortly thereafter from 224 Strand to 226 Strand, it branched out and became a sports store as well as a gun shop with a factory in the basement.

In 1896 the company, obviously regarding itself as providing for outdoor sports and activities of a more diverse nature, designed the Armus bicycle. In the same year, another cycle named the Orpheus was registered. The following year, 1897, saw the patenting of the 'dished gearwheel' and this was offered on all Cogswell & Harrison cycles.

The Feltham factory, built after the 1922 Gillingham Street fire (see page 45), had facilities for the manufacture of sports goods. Cogswell & Harrison itself produced tennis racquets, huge quantities of golf clubs, golf balls and fishing rods. In addition, a number of goods bearing the company name were produced by sub-contractors.

Armus bicycle. The Armus trademark was used for a range of bicycles designed by Edgar Harrison in 1896. Armus was also used for a range of guns produced around the same period.

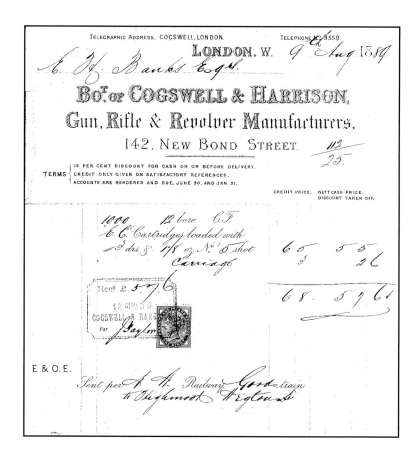

## The Certus Air Pistol

In the late 1920s Edgar Harrison's creative mind was turned to the design of air pistols. This resulted in a provisional specification (No. 330,105) in 1929, which was not consolidated into a full patent. The principle upon which this air pistol works is clear from the drawing on p 73. It is also evident from the drawing that Harrison's design influenced the subsequent development of air pistols and rifles.

While the patent was being pursued, the pistols were being manufactured in small batches. They were advertised in the 1929 catalogue and were available without a stock at 30s. When stocked and supplied in a box with pellets and cleaning equipment the cost was 40s.

Certus pellets were on sale at 2s 6d per thousand. Some were supplied with good quality cases and are now collectors' items. The publicity material with the pistol stated:

*More accurate shooting - perfectly bored and rifled.*
*Breech automatically opened for reloading.*
*When loaded, absolutely safe until breech lever is closed.*
*Certainly unequalled for ease of cocking mainspring.*
*British made throughout.*

# 5  Books and Publications

Those working within a craft tradition do not generally write extensively. More usually, their products speak for themselves. Where books do appear, they are frequently the work of academics, historians, specialist collectors or those interested in craft skills at a particular historical stage.

Whilst there are many such external writers in the case of gunmaking, one is struck by the number of books originating within the tradition itself. W.W. Greener's *The Gun and its Development* was first published in 1881. Nine editions had appeared by 1910. More recently, it was continued with the New Orchard edition published in 1988. Charles Lancaster's *The Art of Shooting* was first published in 1889 and was in its tenth edition by 1942. In the intervening years, many more have appeared. *The Shotgun* by T.D.S and J.A. Purdey appeared in 1936 and Robert Churchill's book *How to Shoot* was published in 1925.

The last two decades have witnessed the publication of books by several of the London houses, which located the company's developments in an historical context: Richard Beaumont's *Purdeys: The Guns and the Family* in 1984, Peter King's *The Shooting Field: 150 Years with Holland and Holland* in 1985 and *Boss, Makers of Best Guns Only* by Donald Dallas in 1996.

Cogswell & Harrison have been involved in publishing since the turn of the nineteenth century. In July 1900 they published *Shooting with Game and Gun Room Notes* by 'Blagdon'. Described as 'A comprehensive book of how to shoot', it addressed topics such as gun fitting, modern guns and ammunition, different forms of live and inanimate bird shooting. The book was illustrated with drawings by Archibald Thorburn, Henry Stannard and others from the *Badminton Magazine* and Hudson's *British Birds*. It included photographs taken at the Blagdon Shooting School. The introduction concluded 'that these pages will produce some interest, and possibly some good effect, is the wish of the writer who adopts the nom de plume of Blagdon'. In reality Blagdon was Edgar Harrison. The book sold for one shilling for the card hardback edition and one shilling and six pence for the cloth board edition.

In 1906 Edgar Harrison embarked upon a more extensive book, *A Dissertation upon Guns and Shooting*. Aware that several books dealing with these topics already existed, he pointed out:

> The author must be prepared to justify his incursion into a field already to a great extent occupied by some special feature or features which will form a differentia between the new aspirant and its predecessors.

Harrison was strongly of the opinion that the good sportsman should not only understand field sport practices and display good field craft together with knowledge of and respect for the quarry but should also understand the technical aspects of the gun he is using:

## SHOOTING.

WITH

### GAME AND GUN-ROOM NOTES.

By " Blagdon."

*A Comprehensive Book of HOW TO SHOOT.*

GUN  FITTING.        GROUSE.
MODERN  GUNS.        PARTRIDGE.
AMMUNITION.        PHEASANT.
LIVE  &  INANIMATE  BIRD  SHOOTING.

Very Extensively Illustrated with Full-Page and Other-sized Drawings
and Photographs from Life.

The Drawings by Archibald Thorburn, Henry Stannard, and Others.

London:
COGSWELL AND HARRISON. Limited.
1900
*(All Rights Reserved.)*

Its differentia is of the highest importance to anyone who aspires to be something more that a casual fair shot. The motorist who is ignorant of the mechanisms of the machine he drives, or the yachtman who knows nothing of seamanship or navigation is not unjustly regarded as a very half hearted devotee of his hobby, but many a man who would claim to be an ardent gunner is surprisingly unversed in the technics of the gun. This is not as it should be, though the omission has perhaps been due to the difficulty of finding a handy and lucid handbook to the science.

The book deals with the concept of quality in a gun, how a gun is made, the art of barrel making, the nature of single triggers and much more. It deals with practices in the field including the use of dogs and describes different forms of gameshooting and wildfowling. It is quite technical in parts and illustrates the Cogswell & Harrison barrel gauge, its plug and ring gauges and apparatus for testing the strength of cartridge turnovers. Remarkably (for that time), it includes photographs of typical cap explosions. With its numerous illustrations including four by J.G. Millais, it is an interesting example of technical description and practical advice for the sporting field.

In 1970, the English Universities Press Ltd, together with Hodder & Stoughton invited the company to produce a book entitled *Shooting* as part of the popular series of 'Teach Yourself' books at that time. This little book contains sections on 'The Gun Dog', 'Before Shooting', 'Gun Safety', 'Full Bore Rifle Shooting', 'Small Bore Rifle Shooting', 'Target Pistol Shooting', 'Ground Shooting', 'Wildfowling' and 'Gameshooting in General'. Many sections were written by Anthony Tucker who was then a Director of Cogswell & Harrison. Both paper and hard cover editions were published with a second edition in 1976.

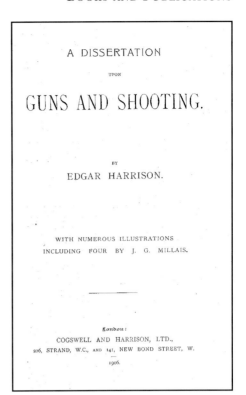

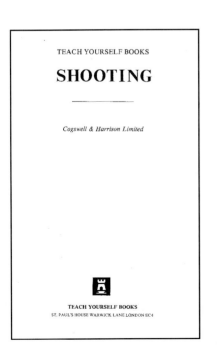

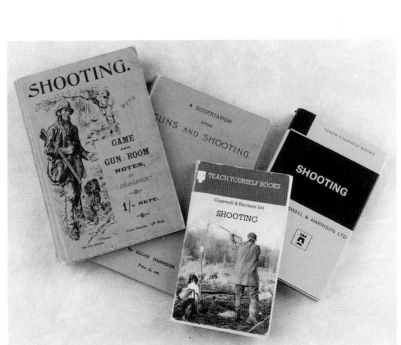

# 6  Surviving the Turbulent Years

In 1932 a new limited company was formed under the direction of Edgar Harrison, John Peskett, M.R. de Cordova and Mr Hazeldine. The old company, also Cogswell & Harrison Ltd. had been put into voluntary liquidation in 1932 to facilitate reorganisation.

This reorganisation enabled the company to consider the purchase of a factory. No suitable premises were available in London and so a site was obtained in Birmingham. It was while in Birmingham that Edgar Harrison had his first heart attack. Following a stay in a nursing home he was back to his gruelling work routine and in 1935 the company purchased its Acton factory, having retained the Piccadilly showrooms during this difficult transitional period.

In 1938, after 42 years as the Chairman of Cogswell & Harrison, Edgar Harrison died. He was succeeded by his son-in-law, Major de Cordova, whose business interests were primarily in Jamaica. The company was effectively run by John Peskett, who was appointed Managing Director and R. Stuart Murray who had been appointed to the Board in 1937.

During the war, the directors were joined by Dorothy Peskett, who came straight from college, and in 1948 she married Ted Holden in Salisbury, Southern Rhodesia. He joined the company in 1950 as the Sales Manager in Piccadilly. During the war he had held the rank of Major in the Indian Army on the Northwest Frontier and later served with the Special Airborne Intelligence Patrol Unit in Burma. Ted Holden had considerable practical knowledge of big game hunting and shooting abroad and this was an asset to the company. Shortly after joining Cogswell & Harrison, he too was made a Director.

In the 1950s the emphasis was on the supply of ex-government rifles and equipment to armed forces all over the world. At this time Mr Samuel Cummings, President of the International Armament Corporation of America and Canada, made an offer to purchase the Cogswell & Harrison shares. At a meeting of the Board, shareholders were advised to accept the offer and in September 1957 the transfer of ordinary shares was made and a majority holding allocated to him.

With capital advanced by Mr. Cummings, a large factory was purchased, the Cannon Works, Bollo Lane, Acton (a different site from the earlier Acton factory) and new plant and extensive equipment was installed. Large quantities of small arms were purchased from the ministries, some individual lots exceeding £250,000 in value.

At this stage Mr Stuart Murray began extensive overseas travels and large orders were secured which enabled Cogswell & Harrison to take over Wright Bros, gunmakers in Birmingham, who for many years had made shotguns for the London

Typical Verey pistol. Thousands were produced by Cogswell & Harrison during the two World Wars.

Photo: David Grant

Plate 1  An Edward Harrison pin-fire 12-bore, No. 5,883, with automatic half-cocking mechanism, the subject of his patent No. 271 of 1 February 1864. *(E. Rosner collection.)*

Plate 2

An Extra Quality Victor model 20-bore boxlock. One of a pair, Nos 80,500/1, completed in 1971 with 26 in. barrels, Churchill ribs, scroll backed action, base plates with retrievers carrying pheasants, 14⁷/8 in. highly figured stocks, weight 5 lb 12 oz. *(Courtesy of Sothebys.)*

A massive 4-bore double rifle/shotgun combination set, No. 15,056, built in 1887. The overall weight was 21 lb 4 oz with the 24 in., 12 lb 3 oz damascus rifle barrels. The 36 in. shotgun barrels were originally BP proofed for 3½ oz of shot. *(Courtesy J.C. Devine Inc.)*

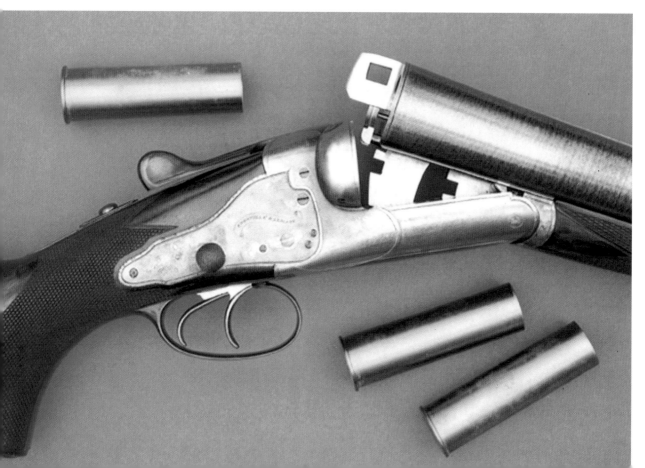

Members of the Board during the period 1930 to 1970. top, l to r: Edgar Harrison, John Peskett, R. Stuart Murray. bottom, l to r: M.R. de Cordova, Ted Holden, H.C. Littlewood.

suppliers. In 1959 Sam Cummings took over Robert Churchill Ltd, the well-known gunmakers of Grange Street, London, the Hercules Arms Company and the Shooting School at Crayford. This was the start of a large combine consisting of Interarmco, Cogswell & Harrison Ltd (including William Moore & Grey), Robert Churchill Ltd, Wright Bros and Charles Boswell Ltd, and by the early 1970s also included Atkin Grant Lang, Beesley, Hellis, Lancaster and Watson Bros.

The principals jointly administered the companies. Stuart Murray and Leonard Pearse, late of Holland and Holland, became Joint Managing Directors of Robert Churchill Ltd and Tom Littlewood was elected Secretary. Stuart Murray succeeded John Peskett as Managing Director of the company Cogswell & Harrison Ltd in 1959, when Peskett went into semi-retirement. Tom Littlewood continued as Secretary. John Peskett, Ted Holden and Tom Littlewood were re-elected Directors of Cogswell & Harrison Ltd.

95% of all weapons handled were exported. The Canadian outlet was huge and on 7 September 1961 the *Acton Gazette and Post* quoted Stuart Murray as having said that the company would buy firearms up to a value of five million pounds if they became available and that a large percentage would go to America. He also made the point in respect of shotguns that in view of the encouragement given by the Government to the shooting of pigeons, the working man was now their best customer and that shooting was no longer confined to the wealthy landowner.

However, it was clear that these activities were drawing the company away from its traditional gunmaking business and thus in March 1963 the retail business, name and goodwill of Cogswell & Harrison was purchased from Sam Cummings and Stuart Murray by John Peskett, Ted Holden and other British shareholders. The workshop was retained by Interarmco., so a new and small workshop premises were rented in Connaught Street and attempts were made to diversify the company's trading base.

Ted Holden entered into a number of overseas government munition contracts, sought overseas agencies for Civil Engineering and sold naval equipment. In 1965 a freehold factory was purchased in Lots Road, Chelsea. It included a contract joinery business that manufactured purpose-made furniture. The joinery business was continued until 1968 and Richard Cooper, an Export Sales Manager, joined the Board.

In March 1969 John Peskett, the Chairman of the company died at the age of 87 and in the sixtieth year of his service with Cogswell & Harrison. In August 1969 Andrew Tucker resigned to form his own business. The Board was then reorganised. Ted Holden was elected Managing Director and Chairman with Dorothy Holden still a Director. Ron Cheesmen was given the title of Export Contracts Director and Richard Cooper, Home Sale Director. Mr C. Street was appointed Company Secretary and Chief Accountant. The following year, in 1970, the Board celebrated its Bicentenary. The company continued trading until it filed for voluntary liquidation in September 1982.

The company was purchased from the liquidator on 25 November 1982 to become Cogwell & Harrison (Shooting Supplies) Ltd. There followed negotiations with Farlows of Pall Mall, London, and in 1983 Farlows announced they had purchased the goodwill of Cogswell & Harrison with the intention of expanding their own increasing sales of shooting accessories. During the period of Farlows' ownership, a gunmaking licence was issued to J. Roberts & Son from 1984 to 1989. The company functioned from Farlows in Pall Mall for the next five years until it was sold to the Cooley family in 1993.

Alan Crewe, Director of Gunmaking, now co-ordinates and inspects the work of various specialists.

Photos: David Clark

# 7 Celebrations: 200 Years of Gunmaking

Both the Board and the Staff can be proud of their service to a Company with such a distinguished history of 200 years. Cogswell & Harrison has met with brilliant success, but has also suffered calamities and, at times, had to overcome disasters which many Company Directors and Staff would not have had the fortitude to face. Death, destruction and financial loss have all struck their blows but, with the will to carry on, Cogswell & Harrison still remain in the forefront of the gun trade. Conscious of the long traditions and a heritage vested in them by so very many past employees, the present-day Board and Staff are determined that the Company will continue to prosper and provide the professional and skilled services required by their customers.

JOHN PESKETT, *Bicentenary of a Gunmaker*

There are not many London gunmakers that have had the opportunity of celebrating their bicentenary and proudly proclaiming '200 years of gunmaking'. In 1970, to mark its 200th birthday, Cogswell & Harrison celebrated in several ways.

In keeping with the company's tradition of encouraging and supporting young sportsmen and women, it established the Perpetual Challenge Cup, 'for boys and girls under the age of 19'. It bears the legend 'Presented by Cogswell & Harrison to commemorate their Bicentenary. The Cogswell & Harrison Perpetual Challenge Cup'.

As no history of the company existed, the bicentenary was a stimulus to produce one. The result was the publication of *Bicentenary of a Gunmaker*. John E. Peskett had been with the company in various administrative capacities from 1908 until his death in 1969, his last ten years being in semi-retirement. The book is described as a brief history of the development of Cogswell & Harrison. It was compiled by colleagues from notes, photographs and illustrations that John Peskett had collected throughout his lifetime.

The Bicentenary was also celebrated by the introduction of three special models: a special version of the Victor sidelock ejector, the Ambassador and the Regency Bicentenary Model. They were together referred to as 'Guns of Distinction'.

The Victor Bicentenary model SLE featured hand-detachable locks and high quality game scene engraving. It was custom built in respect of barrel length, borings and stock dimensions. Chamber lengths in 12 bore were available at 2¾, 2½ or 2 in. A variety of ribs were available including Rib Foulard, Churchill type or raised file-cut.

This fine sidelock was offered at a special commemorative price of £1,050 and delivery was from 12 to 18 months depending on the specification.

The title page of John Peskett's book.

BICENTENARY
*of a*
GUNMAKER

*a collection of notes and illustrations by*
JOHN E. PESKETT

COGSWELL AND HARRISON LTD.
168 PICCADILLY . LONDON W.1

## Perpetual Challenge Cup Winners

| | | | | | |
|---|---|---|---|---|---|
| 1970 | C.J. Noden | 1980 | C.D. Dean | 1990 | W.D. Gibbard |
| 1971 | T. Poskitt | 1981 | P. Mills | 1991 | J.R. Reed |
| 1972 | J. Mason | 1982 | M. Grantham | 1992 | C.N. Apthine |
| 1973 | D.J. Farwell | 1983 | C. Morris | 1993 | A.J. Philpott |
| 1974 | D.J. Farwell | 1984 | S. Whitelock | 1994 | A.J. Philpott |
| 1975 | A.J. Secker | 1985 | R.J. Houghton | 1995 | A.J. Rist |
| 1976 | D.J. Lawton | 1986 | M.N.M. Cook | 1996 | L. Marshall |
| 1977 | K. Bond | 1987 | H. Wild | 1997 | L. Marshall |
| 1978 | R.S. Mowforth | 1988 | P.B. Westall | 1998 | S. Wells |
| 1979 | R.J. Jennings | 1989 | M.T. Keen | 1999 | S. Wells |

## Well Fitted

To celebrate its Bicentenary in 1970, Cogswell & Harrison introduced three special models: the Regency, the Ambassador and a special Victor side-lock ejector. These were referred to as Guns of Distinction. An interesting marketing feature was that the price included a free fitting at the West London Shooting Grounds.

These fittings were inevitably carried out by the legendary Percy Stanbury, the leading coach and member of a team which also included David Bennett, John Mayo, Alan Rose, Michael Rose and David Olive. The *Shooting Times* described him as, 'Perhaps one of the most famous shots of this era'. Peter Page, then Director of the Clay Pigeon Shooting Association (CPSA) said: 'Percy Stanbury completely dedicated to the sport of shooting, is one of the most

effective coaches ever and is well renowned for his ability to impart his knowledge of shooting to other people. He has a kind word for everybody and is one of the most cheerful and unassuming sportsmen I know.'

Percy Stanbury represented his country in the English International Team on 26 occasions and was the high gun on four of them. He was the core author with Major Gordon Carlisle of three excellent books about shooting: *Shotgun Marksmanship*, *Shotgun and Shooter* and *Clay Pigeon Marksmanship*.

Sportsmen from all over the world benefitted from Percy's coaching skills. The company records include information on those who bought one of the 'guns of distinction' and thoroughly enjoyed their gunfitting and coaching session with Percy.

Courtesy of *The Shooting Times*

Coaches at the West London Shooting Grounds (l to r): David Bennett, John Mayo, Percy Stanbury, Alan Rose, Michael Rose and David Olive.

The Piccadilly shop front converted to celebrate the bicentenary of 1970.

The Regency was a high quality handmade boxlock hammerless ejector. It had a scroll back action and featured deep scroll engraving, gold plated triggers and the rib bore the name 'Regency' inlaid in gold. The gun had excellent handling characteristics and if 26 in. barrels were chosen it weighed typically 6¼ lbs. It was also custom built and was priced at £500. The guns were popular and there was a brisk market for them.

By the mid 1970s the price still included free fitting at the West London Shooting Grounds plus insurance for one year with delivery at 12 to 18 months. The 12-bore Regency was then selling at £1,295 whilst the Victor started at £2,750 and with detachable locks at £3,500.

Advertisement for the Regency, Ambassador and Victor from *Shooting Times & Country Magazine*, 19-25 August 1976.

### PEDIGREE GUNS of DISTINCTION !

**The Regency**    **The Ambassador**

Cogswell & Harrison model Ambassador boxlock ejector. With ornamental side plates. Superb gun. With choice of game scene or rose scroll engraving. Gold triggers. Free fitting at West London Shooting Grounds.

12 BORE £1500
16 BORE £1550
20 BORE £1575

This hand-made model incorporates a superior grade boxlock and other outstanding features such as deep scroll engraving set into a polished action, gold-plated triggers and inlaid gold rib. It has been highly commended for its superb balance and handling qualities. Includes free fitting at West London Shooting Grounds and free insurance for one year. Barrels 26in, 28in, 30in. Chambers 2½in. Chokings as required.

DELIVERY 12 to 18 MONTHS, BUT PRICES WILL STAND AS THOSE RULING AT TIME OF ORDER

12 BORE £1295
16 BORE £1350
20 BORE £1377

ALL PRICES INCLUDE VAT
WE SUPPLY AN EXPERT REPAIRS SERVICE AT REASONABLE PRICES

**The VICTOR**

The Cogswell & Harrison 12 bore "Victor" Sidelock Ejector is a product of the best in British Gunmaking, backed by 200 years of experience. It is made to order for the sportsman who puts perfection before price. Detachable Locks made to order, which can be removed in a few seconds. Triggers double or single. Barrels 25in, 26in or 28in. Chambers 2½in, 2½in or 2in. Chokings as required. Rib-Foulard, "Churchill" type or raised file-cut. Free insurance for one year. Free fitting at West London Shooting Grounds. £2,750

With detachable lock £3,500

**COGSWELL & HARRISON LTD**
168 PICCADILLY · LONDON · W1 · Tel: 01-493-4746/01-629-5923

# 8  Pedigree and Provenance: The Cogswell & Harrison Archive

Cogswell & Harrison, and particularly Edgar Harrison, always prided themselves on maintaining meticulous records of the thousands of guns that have found their way to every corner of the globe. When they return for regulation or restoration as they regularly do, their history can be retold from the stock books. Despite the destruction of so much source material in the various disasters which befell the company, most of the archive record books giving details of the handmade shotguns and rifles have, amazingly survived to the present day.

If you buy a handmade London gun you can usually find out a lot about it by contacting the maker. Company records describe, often in considerable detail, the original specification of the gun. By quoting the serial number the company can usually tell you the year your gun was built, to whom it was sold and for how much. If you are considering buying a pre-owned gun you can check if it is original by comparing its weight and dimensions with the recorded ones.

Well-kept records usually indicate whether the gun has been returned for repair or has been re-sold by the company. Each gun has its own pedigree and the records are valuable provenance. However company policy differs and some makers are loath to reveal this provenance, taking the view that the information is the private affair of the original owner. Some other makers take the view that the principle of provenance should be applied to handmade shotguns and rifles like the deeds of a house or the logbook of a classic car. This is the position taken by Cogswell & Harrison.

The Cogswell & Harrison records are accessed via four index volumes indicating on which page of which archive book the original records are to be found. The archive books consist of fifteen huge volumes each containing over 1000 pages. The books are fragile and in a distressed condition and only consulted when the owner of a Cogswell & Harrison shotgun or rifle requests details under a particular serial number.

It has unfortunately been necessary to refuse requests from interested parties to study the books as they must not be opened more than necessary. They still bear the marks of a flood in the office prior to the turn of the last century. A fire destroyed the records of some double rifles but in general the specification of most rifles and shotguns exists.

The information is partially coded but once deciphered is very comprehensive. The date on which work commenced, the model, details of the action, the ejectors and the forend fixing mechanism are all included. The stock length with the bends at the comb and the heel together with the three points of cast-off (or cast-on) are all usually recorded.

The more expensive guns from around 1885 were regulated or at least tested for a particular size and load of shot. Where no shot size or weight was given, it was a $1^{1}/_{8}$ oz load of no. 6 shot. Two figures were given: for example, 139 on the right and 172 on the left indicated the average number of pellets delivered into a 30 in. circle

Archive books including 20
volumes of records. The most
distressed have been restored
in an ongoing process.

Bookcase by Charles Webb.

Photo: David Grant

at 40 yd. When on the other hand the figure on the right was greater than the figure on the left, it indicated the reverse chokes of a driven game gun. The front trigger fired the right barrel as usual, but in this case it was more heavily choked than the left one fired by the back trigger.

The length and weight of the barrels when struck up and ready to fit to the action are given as is the overall weight of the finished gun. Sometimes, separate records indicate in greater detail the form and extent of engraving and whether this had been customised for the requirements of a particular order. The original purchaser, the date of purchase and the price paid would likewise be stated. They also show if the gun was one of a matched pair, composed pair or trio.

The books may also be read as a form of social history and often help to consolidate family records. For example, where guns have been inherited it can be confirmed which member of the family purchased them in the first place. Sometimes, the

## Cogswell & Harrison

Sales and Workshop:
Heathcliffe Parkers Lane
Maidens Green Bracknell
Berks RG42 6LE

Tel: 01344 885091
Fax: 01344 890906

Office:
Thatcham House
95 Sussex Place
Slough
Berks SL1 1NN

Tel: 01753 520866
Fax: 01753 575770

(Gunmakers) Ltd.,

### Certificate of Origin
#### Shotgun No. 40521

*Our craftsmen commenced work on this shotgun on 8th May 1906. It was the third of three guns built to the same specification and with successive numbers. It was a 'T 108' twelve bore double barrel side-by-side boxlock with Avant Tout ejectors and assisted opening mechanism. It was finished as a "Modele de-Luxe" pigeon gun with bold scroll engraving throughout the action and on the sideplates. It was fitted with a conventional top lever, double triggers and a non-automatic top safety. It was equipped with a concealed cross bolt and side clips. The forend had an Anson type fastener.*

*The barrels were 30" long, made of Arcus steel and when completed with a file cut flat rib they weighed 3lb 10oz. Both barrels were bored with thirty-one points of choke i.e approximately three quarters choke in each. They were nitro-proved for $1\frac{1}{4}$ oz and were regulated for no.6 shot. The right barrel then delivered an average of 223 pellets into the 30" circle and the left delivered an average of 226.*

*The stock was $14\frac{1}{2}$" long with the bend at the comb $1\frac{7}{16}$" and at the heel 2". The stock cast offs were respectively $\frac{1}{8}$", $\frac{3}{16}$" and $\frac{1}{4}$". The finished gun weighed 7lb 6oz. On 11th November 1907 the gun was sold to Ketchum & Co for an unnamed original owner who paid thirty-five guineas for it.*

*We confirm that the above information was extracted from the archives of Cogswell & Harrison on 25th February 2000 for the current owner Major R.E. Jones.*

Prof MJE Cooley
Chairman

Reg No: 1638115

RFD: TVD 71

VAT No 366 2798 11

ESTABLISHED 1770

A certificate of provenance.

current owner will say that the year of delivery coincided with his grandfather's 21st birthday and must have been a birthday present. This custom was quite common in many better-off families.

Some of the less expensive boxlocks have passed through three generations of one family giving each the pleasure of ownership and becoming part of the family's heritage. Details from the records can also become part of the family folklore. In 1996 for example, Cogswell & Harrison was contacted by a gentleman in a senior position in the navy whose grandfather had won his gun in a card game on a ship travelling to India in 1910. He was keen to know who lost possession of the gun in that fateful gamble.

At other periods in history, the records can make very sad reading. The 1913 and early 1914 records show many guns being ordered by men who did not take possession of them. From their titles it is clear that some were already army officers.

Although no mention is made of the Great War, the fact that on many occasions a weapon would be sold by Cogswell & Harrison on behalf of a woman with the same surname as the owner, is an illustration of the great tragedy that befell a generation of young men.

# Part Two: Factories, Shooting Grounds and Shops

# 9 Factories and Workshops

For many years Cogswell & Harrison had by far the most extensive and best equipped workshops in the London Gun Trade. Factories at Harrow and Gillingham Street just behind Victoria Station incorporated state of the art technology.

## The Harrow Factory

Edgar Harrison took out his first lease on a large factory in Harrow on the Ferndale Estate in 1886 and then a new lease in 1887 when he was in a revived partnership with the site owner. Experience gained in making the Desideratum hammerless gun was being used there. In an 1879 advertisement the Company prefigured these techniques by stating:

> Cogswell & Harrison, having laid down special machinery for the manufacture of these guns, are in a position to turn them out in a superior style. A judicious admixture of hand labour is used for the fitting of the parts and the shaping of the iron and wood thus ensuring accurate fixing and symmetrical appearance throughout.

It was also at Harrow that facilities existed for what in those days was an acceptable practice - the shooting of live pigeons and starlings. Many sportsmen participated in competitions and practice there. They were encouraged to use Cogswell & Harrison guns and those who had already placed orders were invited to see their own guns in various stages of manufacture.

The factory proved successful at several levels. The introduction of new forms of manufacturing technology and work practices together with the establishment of an important public relations and marketing role for the company foretold a bright future for Cogswell & Harrison. All this however was short-lived as a disastrous fire broke out at 2 am on 16 July 1894. It was suggested at the time that sparks from a locomotive on the adjacent railway line fell through a gap in the factory roof and ignited some shavings.

The machine shop in 1886.

## The Gillingham Street Factory

In consequence of this fire and also as a result of expanding business, new premises were acquired at 29a Gillingham Street, just behind Victoria Station in London. For the next 30 years these were to house the company's main manufacturing facilities. Cogswell & Harrison eventually purchased the extensive premises and erected an up-to-date factory on the site

together with an indoor shooting range. Underground was a tunnel, 150 yards in length, for testing rifles and a rifle range with movable targets and a plating wall.

Joseph Lang claimed he originated the shooting range idea with the gallery at the back of his Haymarket premises in 1827. However, he appears to have been preceded by Joseph Manton who had one in operation in 1814 at the rear of his Davis Street premises.

The facility in Gillingham Street incorporated a main office, general offices and repair workshops. On the ground floor there were the cartridge loading rooms in which (to quote Peskett) 'several hundred girls rolled paper tubes for cartridge making'. It was also there that components such as caps and wadding were made and finally assembled. There was also a section that housed the production of metallic cartridges. At right angles to these rooms were the drying rooms, powder chamber, the machine shops and barrel-boring machines.

The company then had its own powder mills. The laboratories were adjacent to the main building where numerous chemists were employed. Explosives were registered as the 'Fusilite' in 1900, the 'Kelor' Explosive substances in 1907 and the 'Markoroid' Explosive substances in 1908.

By 1900 the gunmaking facilities there were impressive and it was referred to as The Small Arms Factory. It was truly a 'state of the art' facility in terms of those days and the Editor of *The Field* declared it a 'Modern gun factory – the work there produced being unsurpassed by anything in the market'. The Company described the factory as containing 'a complete plant of the latest pattern of high class machinery and appliances so as to turn out the highest class of work'.

It was here that Edgar Harrison sought to demonstrate a symbiosis of hand craftsmanship and the judicious use of machinery. The plant was also unusual in having a design department. The method of manufacture was described in six stages: Design, Modelling, Tooling, Examination (gauging), Materials and Manufacturing.

These modern production techniques were deployed to produce the less expensive boxlock models in the Avant Tout range. G.T. Teasdale-Buckell in *Experts on Guns and Shooting* describes his discussion with Harrison about this facility and asked if such machinery would not eliminate skilled London gunmakers. Harrison asserted that this was not at all the case for these facilities would allow them to use their skills much more effectively by producing components in what would nowadays be called 'Close to Form Technology'. The highly skilled work would still be left to the

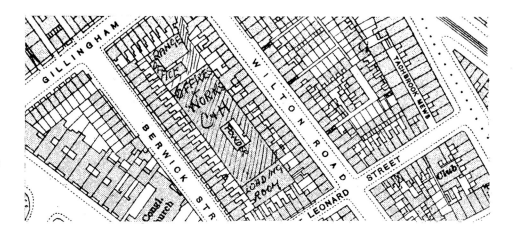

Plan of the Gillingham Street factory site, showing houses evacuated during the fire of 1922.

## The Wealdstone Football Club

Throughout often difficult times, the morale of Cogswell & Harrison employees remained high. Despite long hours, hard work and poor conditions, co-operation between management and staff was excellent. Low ceilings, gloomy gas lighting and the constant whirling noise from shafting was combined with the screech of milling machines and lathes. Through pride in their craft, confidence in the company and a wealth of good humour, Cogswell & Harrison's staff maintained a high level of output and quality unsurpassed by other gunmakers of those Victorian and Edwardian days.

As an example of their spirit, the Harrow employees became the pioneers of organised football in the area laying the basis in 1890 for what is now known as the Wealdstone Football Club. We can sense the size and camaraderie of the Harrow staff since Cogswell & Harrison was able to muster two teams: the Works Team and a team called 'The Oaks' made

up from its clerical staff. Edgar Harrison, who at the time lived in Hindes Road, Harrow actively supported the football activities of the Company and patronised the club. A foreman called Mr Meadows was elected Secretary.

Two games between the Works Team and the Oaks were played on 19 November and 3 December 1887. The Oaks won the first 3-0 and also the return match 1-0 on Cogswell & Harrison's own ground. The enthusiasm and commitment of both teams was exemplary. Mr. Simons, who had joined the Works Team in 1877 at the age of 19 wrote:

> We had a fixture at Hayes and on this particular occasion we started off in our horse-brake without one of our best players. We expected to have to play with a man short but to our surprise, the missing player arrived at the ground five minutes after we did. He had run and walked across country all the way from Harrow to Hayes and then played as good a game as usual.

| The Oaks Team: | T. Hole; S. Gill; W. Stephenson; G. Browne; W. Parker; H. Darville; H. Jones; A. Norris; S. Matthews; H. Waghorn; J. Poole |
|---|---|
| C&H Works Team: | F. Hughes; C. White; G. Norton; J. Walker; T. Blake; G. Gibson; S. Simons; J. Collins; T. Smallwood; G. Dickenson; A.Norman |

craftsman. He declared 'It is the last cut of the file that requires the most judgement and the last cut still remains'.

Teasdale-Buckell points out that by using these techniques 'it enables Cogswell & Harrison to sell a sound London made hammerless ejector gun for fifteen guineas'. He could see that Harrison was anticipating changes in society where shooting would be more democratically based and would be undertaken by a much wider spectrum of society. He pointed out, 'There is a large and growing class of shooters who prefer to pay less than the price charged for first quality guns'. At the time, Cogswell & Harrison charged 59 guineas for one of its best sidelock ejectors. These continued to be made by traditional means and were truly bespoke Best London guns, such as the Extra Quality Victor SLE.

The new production techniques and the associated quality control mechanisms with their specialist equipment were dedicated to the Avant Tout models. Teasdale-Buckell points out 'every part of which except the tubes is manufactured in Gillingham Street close to Victoria'. Some factory facilities existed at the Malden Shooting Grounds and there was also the powder mill at Colnbrook but the focal point of manufacturing was at Gillingham Street and was pivotal to the Company's activities.

It was a truly catastrophic event for Cogswell & Harrison when on 6 May 1922 the Gillingham Street factory was destroyed by fire (ironically, the same fate as had befallen the Harrow factory nearly three decades earlier). The Fire Brigade made every effort to bring the flames under control but the fire raged so fiercely that three adjacent streets had to be evacuated. Not only was the whole building gutted and destroyed but many fine guns and rifles, some of which were the property of customers were also destroyed. Valuable records and drawings were lost which means that some of the records currently lodged with the Company have small gaps in them particularly details of a few rifles. However, the records still contain lists of shotguns and rifles burned in the factory fire.

But that was not all. As Peskett points out, another almost mortal blow was struck when only £34,000 was recovered in insurance against an estimated loss of £65,000 and the company had somehow to make good the difference.

## The Feltham Factory

Great courage and commitment was displayed in redeeming the position after the fire. It was decided almost straight away that a site had to be located and a new factory set up. Eventually, a suitable site was discovered at Feltham; the factory built there was again substantial and the facilities on site included some machinery for the manufacture of sports goods, including tennis racquets under the name of 'C&H Sports' and 'DeCordova & Harrison'.

The primary activity was of course gunmaking. Specialist equipment and machine tools were installed. In a remarkably short length of time the factory was functionng 'at full swing' and the 1923 catalogue refers to it as The Small Arms Factory. Work was undertaken there on one of the most comprehensive range of guns in the company's history.

It ranged from Model De Luxe sidelock ejectors, Victor sidelock ejectors, the new Tower gun, the Crown model and boxlocks including the Sandhurst and the Rex. Cosmos ball and shot guns were included in the range together with high velocity double and magazine rifles. There were rook and rabbit rifles both in side-lever hammer form and hammerless top-lever ejector ones. Double barrel .410 guns were offered in both hammer and hammerless actions with top levers as were .410 walking stick guns which sold with removable butt and safety bolt at five guineas. The new 14 bore (as distinct from 14¾ bore!) ejector guns were produced there. They were available in the Victor model at 100 guineas, the Tower at 70 guineas, the Crown at 40 guineas and the Sandhurst at 30 guineas. A short batch of Moorgrey guns (see page 80) were also made there.

At one stage the Feltham factory was also the location of what might be called the company's 'nerve centre'. Edgar Harrison had a small administrative office there from which he essentially directed the company's overall activities and letters on the 'Small Arms Factory' headed paper and signed by Edgar Harrison went forth to the Piccadilly office, to 94 Queen Street Exeter and to 26 Avenue de l'Opéra in Paris.

## The Acton Factories

Between 1933 and 1935, premises in Birmingham were used until, as a result of reorganisation and available funds, factory premises were acquired in Acton in 1935 and manufacturing remained in Acton for the next 22 years.

On the outbreak of war, the production effort of the company was re-focussed, including the production of spares for rifles and Sten guns. An estimated million and a half parts were processed and six thousand tons of Sten components. When the

The Cannon Works at Acton.

plea went out for guns and rifles to equip the Home Guard, John Peskett and Stuart Murray were requested by the Home Office to tour all the London police head-quarters to examine weapons and decide upon their safety and serviceability. Literally thousands upon thousands of weapons were inspected.

The first Acton works escaped major damage during the war years and production continued in the post war period. The second Cogswell & Harrison Acton Factory was the Cannon Works at Bollo Lane. When in 1967 Cogswell & Harrison again became separate from the combine set up in 1957 by Sam Cummings, it was without its own workshop because the Acton works were retained by the combine (see page 48). A small workshop was therefore rented by Cogswell & Harrison in Connaught Street in the West End of London.

## Park Road Works, Acton

We have described elsewhere the company's contribution to the war effort. A significant part of this work was undertaken at the factory at 21 Park Road, East Acton, London W3. This works was allocated an ordnance contractor's code S 171. The S indicated it was a Southern contractor.

On 24 June 1939 Cogswell & Harrison were awarded a contract to convert 14,323 No. 1 rifles to war readiness standard (WRS). Just prior to that, on 17 June 1939, Cogswell & Harrison was given a contract to break up 3,813 No. 3 and pattern 1917 rifles for spares. Throughout this period, the company produced parts, including spare foresights for the No. 3 rifle. It also produced rifles for special purposes. On 12 March 1942, the company was given a contract to produce 496 .303 No. 1 SMLE (short magazine Lee Enfield) rifles in the assembly/stripped DP (Drill Purposes) form. They were sectioned to show their internal workings and were used to train armourers and others.

Cogswell & Harrison also made sear springs for the .303 Lee Enfield No. 4 rifle and they heat treated the sears for the Lancaster machine carbine used by the Royal Navy.

A special 4 in. smoke discharger was designed and manufactured in large numbers for tanks and armoured vehicles.

The company had extensive facilities in the plant and in the post war period described them as follows: Rifle Manufacturers, Shotgun Manufacturers, Case Hardening, barrel browning and oil blacking. The company also offered a precision engineering service.

Throughout the war period and in fact for some years thereafter, Cogswell & Harrison were contractors to the Ministry of Supply, the War Office and the Admiralty. During this period the company also participated in wider trade associations and government schemes and had membership of the Federation of British Industry (FBI) and took part in a national scheme for disabled men.

The factory at East Acton continued into the 1950s, until the President of the International Arms Corporation of America had purchased the ordinary shares of Cogswell & Harrison and advanced capital for the purchase in 1957 of the factory at Cannon Works, Bollo Lane in Acton.

## Lots Road, Chelsea, London

When the business was purchased back from Interarms Ltd in March 1963, the factory in Acton was retained by Interarms Ltd. As an interim arrangement a small workshop was rented in Connaught Street. This sufficed for a couple of years. However, in 1965 a large order (one of the largest single orders in the company's history) was successfully concluded.

At that time a freehold factory was purchased at 91-93 Lots Road, Chelsea. The facilities there included a joinery business. This, together with the manufacture of purpose-made furniture and contract joinery work was continued until 1968. From a gunmaking point of view there were a number of interesting developments at Lots Road. A 12-bore starting pistol was successfully developed and the repeating flare signal pistol was designed at that stage. Prototypes were produced in 1968 and the starting pistol went into production in 1969.

In the post war period substantial trade work was done for Cogswell & Harrison by J. Blanch & Sons who also undertook work for companies in the Churchill, Atkin Grant & Lang group. At one stage Blanch actually operated from Cogswell & Harrison's Lots Road premises. During this period, Blanch purchased guns 'in the white' from Cogswell & Harrison. These guns bore Cogswell & Harrison serial numbers in the 70000 range rather than Blanch's own numbers. In fact to this day, Cogswell & Harrison has gun components and accessories and one or two guns in the white which were destined for J. Blanch & Sons.

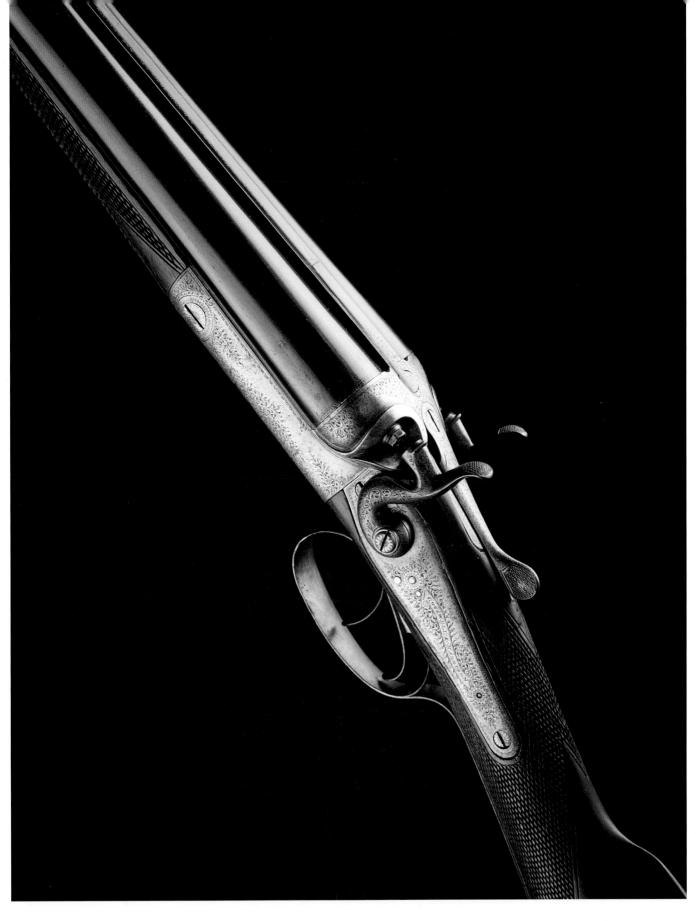

Plate 3  Work commenced on this 12-bore hammer ejector shotgun No. 14,742 on 13 July 1887. The extra cost of incorporating the ejectors was six guineas. *(E. Rosner collection.)*

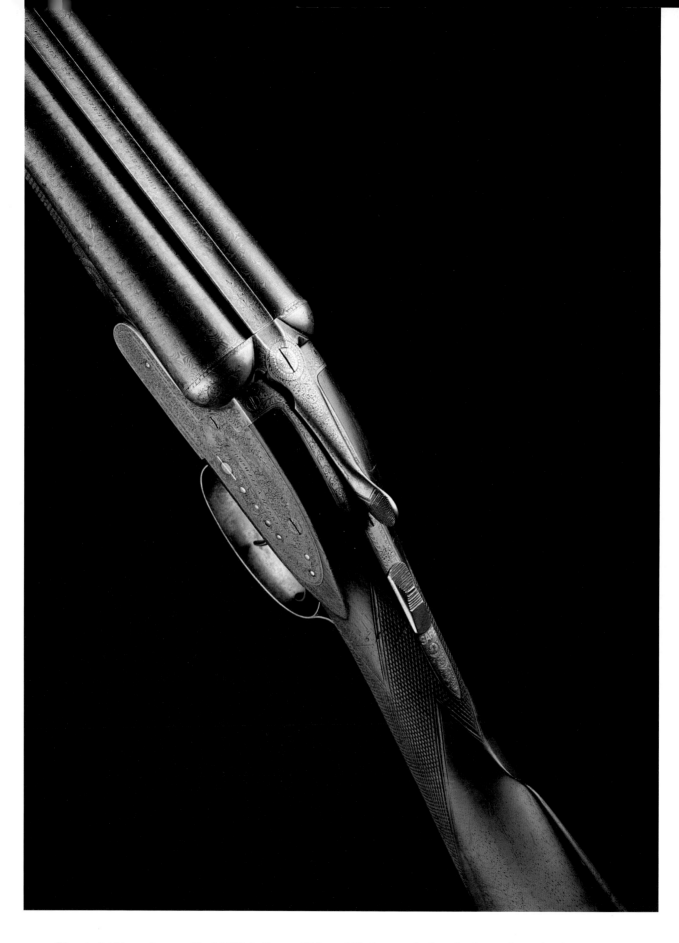

Plate 4  A 12-bore shotgun, No. 11,689, built on a Gibbs and Pitt lever cocked mechanism and completed on
26 September 1882. Note the top automatic *reverse* safety. *(E. Rosner collection.)*

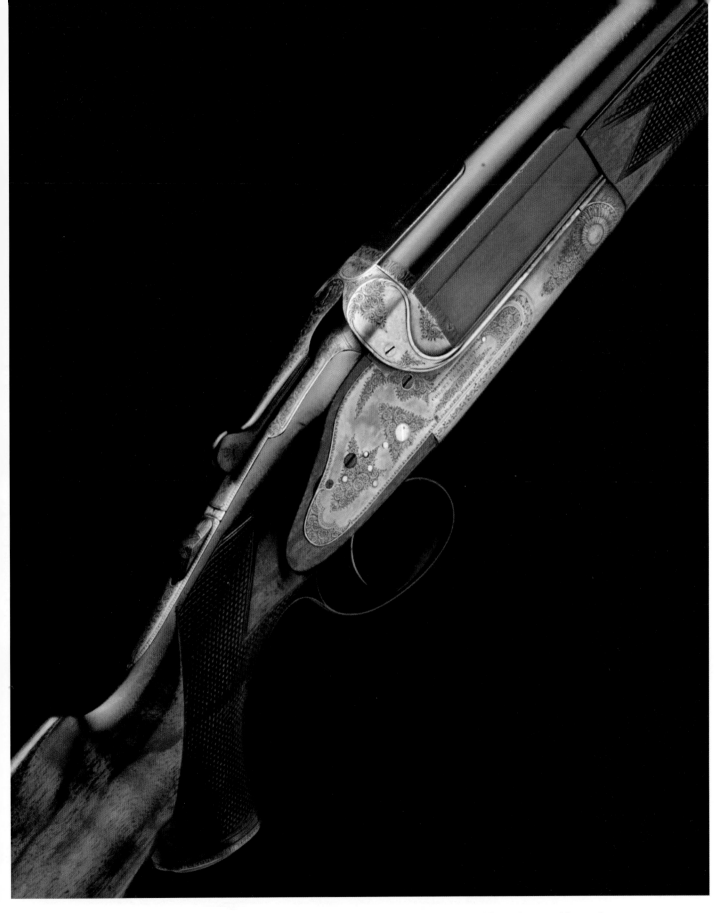

Plate 5  A 4-bore single barrel sidelock hammerless non-ejector, No. 11,645, built in 1882 with top lever cocking and automatic safety. The 42 in. damascus barrel with a 4 in. chamber was bored full choke. The overall weight was 13 lb 14 oz.
*(Courtesy of Bonhams.)*

Plate 6 (top) A type 123 .475 double rifle, No. 42,673, No. 1 of a pair with No. 42,674 and (bottom) a .375 double rifle No. 42,714, No. 1 of a pair with No. 42,715. Both pairs were delivered to the original owner, for whom they were custom built, on 31 December 1908. *(J. Kilday collection.)*

A 16-bore, assisted opening, rotary underlever, ejector hammergun, No. 22,941, built to customer specification and delivered on 21 November 1895. The 24 in. damascus barrels were nitroproofed for 2¾ in. chambers in 1990. *(Courtesy N. Holt & Co.)*

# 10  Shooting Grounds and Schools

At the turn of the century, there were some twenty shooting schools in and around London. Many of them were set up and owned by individual gunmakers and used exclusively by their customers for practice, testing and gun fitting. In some cases schools did not limit themselves to owners of their own company's guns. Gun fitting and specifying dimensions for the manufacture of bespoke guns was often carried out for other, perhaps smaller gunmakers. There were also several independent shooting schools catering for the general public and used by a number of gunmakers. Finally, there were shooting grounds and clubs, which were not shooting schools as such but rather facilities for practice and competition.

Cogswell & Harrison had two shooting schools one at Colnbrook called the Cogswell & Harrison Shooting Park and the other at Malden in Surrey, which was known as the Blagdon Shooting Grounds.

## The Cogswell & Harrison Shooting Park, Colnbrook

The shooting school at Colnbrook was located close to what was then Colnbrook station, just a short distance west of the present day London Heathrow Airport and a 30-minute journey from London on the Great Western Railway. It was established in the 1880s and an advertisement in 1888 shows that it was by then well established with a 'rocketing pheasant' high tower to simulate pheasants over high trees.

To quote contemporary documents Cogswell & Harrison provided practice for every kind of sporting shot: realistic covert; well arranged partridge drives etc. A special feature of the school was gun fitting and shooting lessons by experienced coaches. It was an all-embracing facility and at the time *The Field* observed, 'At Colnbrook, everything necessary to the shooter is to hand'.

A cautionary note, from *Shooting* by 'Blagdon'.

The company had an aggressive marketing policy, for those days. It encouraged a wide clientele and proudly proclaimed that Cogswell & Harrison's or other makers' guns may be used. Everything was done to facilitate the transport of the clients to the shooting school. The company had its own fleet of cars and would transport shooters to and from a number of local stations including those on the Southern Region and Great Western Railways. Collections were also made from local towns such as Eton and Windsor or 'any place within the district of Colnbrook'. In July 1912, the cost of this chauffeur driven service was 1s 6d.

Safe        Dangerous!        Safe

## Try-Guns

It is not surprising that with its extensive involvement in shooting schools, Cogswell & Harrison should have developed its own Try Gun. Gun fitting, as distinct from practice and coaching was emphasised by the company at its shooting grounds under the banner: 'To shoot well, use a good fitting gun'.

The company encouraged sportsmen and women to avail themselves of the facilities at its Blagdon fitting range in Malden and also in Colnbrook. The company stated in its 1900 catalogue: 'Visitors to our fitting ranges can always ensure the services of Fitters who are specialists of the first order and permanently attached to the fitting ranges.'

The Cogswell & Harrison Try-Gun allowed for 'any length, inclination of the heel plate, bend and cast-off to be obtained'. It was of rigid construction and once it had been adjusted it could be locked quite rigidly. For example, two joints instead of one were employed for the lateral movement of the stock. Furthermore, once adjusted and fixed to suit a particular sportsman it could be used in the field as any other sporting gun.

Illustrations were made to show the effect of insufficient cast-off and too much bend in the stock. There were illustrations of a stock being too straight with insufficient cast-on and finally, the well centred pattern of a correct fit.

*It is the first principle in stock fitting that the gun must be made to come up correctly at once without requiring any readjustment before firing.*

Once the correct dimensions had been obtained, the company provided a service to modify the sportsman's existing gun to an appropriate 'fit'. The try guns were used of course to get the correct dimensions for customers ordering a Cogswell & Harrison gun. In this case the service was free. Where dimensions were being provided for another gunmaker to build a new gun, the charge for the fitting session in 1900 was 10s 6d.

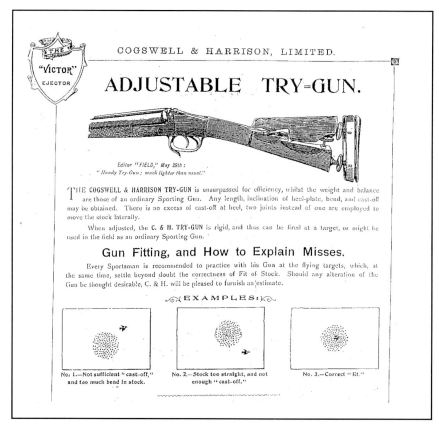

Advertisement from the Cogswell & Harrison catalogue of 1900.

Gun fitting sessions, including the use of an adjustable try-gun and cartridges together with the services of an experienced gun fitter, was 10s 6d. Practice with full use of the grounds and attendance for two hours was 7s 6d. Cartridges or 'Swiftsure' inanimate birds were supplied at the rate of 8s 4d per hundred. Season tickets were also available at special prices for pre-payment. A practice subscription entitling the subscriber to an unlimited number of visits for twelve months was £2 2s 0d (two guineas).

An unlimited number of lessons and practice for twelve months with 500 cartridges and birds was five guineas. Special rates were provided for 'juveniles', i.e. £2 12s 6d for five lessons including the use of a good coach and 100 cartridges and birds for each lesson.

Colnbrook was also the location of the ammunition factory and the smokeless powder factory. Cogswell Harrison's early death in the 1915 explosion at the powder mills was the event which led to the abrupt closure of the shooting school and the disposal of the Colnbrook facility altogether (see page 116).

## Blagdon Shooting School

The Blagdon Shooting School was located near Malden in Surrey. There were frequent trains from London to Raynes Park and Malden, both three-quarters of a mile from the grounds, or Wimbledon Station, which was two miles away. All the facilities described in respect of the Colnbrook Shooting School were available at Blagdon. It was in a beautiful location with a large wooded area known as Blagdon Woods. Many additional facilities were provided which we now associate with modern shooting schools. The Editor of *The Field* observed, 'Expansive grounds, beautifully wooded. Practice at every kind of shooting. Elegantly appointed public, luncheon and ladies' rooms'.

Apart from the usual clientele of 'sportsmen' the company was also keen to encourage visits to the school in the form of family outings. For example, it provided six sets of shooting lessons with practice and a good coach for all the brothers of one family at five guineas. Advertising emphasised special arrangements for ladies. Advertisements stated, 'Ladies and Gentlemen can form their own parties at Blagdon. Every accommodation is offered including luncheons and other meals etc provided in the House or on the shoot.'

The Marquess of Cranby declared on 4 July 1898 that Blagdon was 'A most excellent place for the purpose of trying one's guns'. The *Shooting Times* said it 'comes nearest our ideal'.

The shooting grounds inevitably reflected the norms and standards of society at that time. There were many clubs around London where competitions

Advertisement for the Blagdon Shooting School from 1900.

# 'Blagdon' Shooting School

(Frequent trains to Malden or Raynes Park Station, ¾ mile; also Wimbledon Station, 2 miles).

## GUN FITTING by SPECIALISTS

At BLAGDON (open-air range); or in LONDON (enclosed range).

*The Most Hon. the MARQUIS OF GRANBY :—" . . Thoroughly practical and convenient."*

TO SHOOT WELL, USE A GOOD-FITTING GUN.

"BLAGDON" OPEN-AIR RANGE;

"LONDON" ENCLOSED RANGE.

THE GUN STOCK OF EVERY SPORTSMAN SHOULD FIT TO A NICETY SHOULD HE WISH TO SHOOT HIS BEST.

*Editor FIELD :—" An exceedingly ingenious principle. Handy Try-gun, much lighter than usual."*

### *Shooting Lessons by Expert Instructors*

*COUNTY GENTLEMAN :—" The best of such Schools."*

At Blagdon the services of an experienced Coach are always obtainable to give advice to those sportsmen who require tuition in the art of Shooting.

A series of visits will enable the young shooter, or one who has commenced later in life, to have confidence in the field, and necessarily a greater average of kills to his credit.

**UNLIMITED PRACTICE.**
Season's Subscription Tickets now issued, 2 Guineas net.

and shoots were held with live pigeons as targets. We would correctly find such practices unacceptable today but the Blagdon Grounds also provided such facilities. Whilst it advertised the inanimate 'Swiftsure' birds trapped per hundred at £10 6s, it also advertised live pigeons trapped per dozen at 18s and live pigeons – better quality trapped per dozen at £1 1s. By special arrangement rabbits could be released at 18s per dozen with starlings per dozen at 6s. Gradually, the use of live birds was replaced with inanimate targets giving realistic simulation for various kinds of gameshooting. It was one of the first to provide training schemes for specialist staff.

These shooting grounds were an important part of the company's development. During this period the company developed its own try guns with special stocks. Peskett pointed out, 'The shooting schools had enabled the company to train expert gunfitters thus combining a knowledge of firearms with practical appreciation of sporting conditions'.

A number of those associated with the Blagdon Shooting School went on to make considerable reputations in their own right. The manager of the grounds for a period up to about October 1901 was Mr Richmond-Watson. He was keen to develop a business of his own and, initially, entered into negotiations with Joseph Lang. For some unstated reason the negotiations were not satisfactory and Richmond-Watson set up his own shooting grounds at Perivale, Ealing. Eventually, in 1931 he moved from there to the West London Shooting Grounds in Northolt. To this day, the Richmond-Watson family manages these grounds.

Cogswell & Harrison retained its contact with the WLSG over many years and at one stage advertised the prices of all its new guns to include gunfitting at the West London Shooting Grounds. Many Cogswell & Harrison owners throughout the world are still using guns fitted at the West London Shooting Grounds with dimensions provided by the famous Percy Stanbury.

Advertisement for the Colnbrook Shooting Grounds, from *Guns and Shooting* by Edgar Harrison, published by Cogswell & Harrison in 1906.

# 11  The Paris Connection

At the turn of the century most British companies were still concentrating their export efforts on the British Empire and the English-speaking world. In addition to being actively involved in these markets, Cogswell & Harrison was conscious of the potential of markets in continental Europe, the entry into Europe being via Paris.

For a period of 30 years the company had an elaborate and elegant Paris shop with showrooms at 26 Avenue de l'Opéra. It was opened in 1901 and flourished under the patronage of HRH the Duke of Orleans, becoming a fashionable centre for French sportsmen. The Paris shop offered the whole range of Cogswell & Harrison products. Bespoke guns and Double Rifles were ordered there and produced in London to the customer's specific requirements. Later the Company opened a shooting school outside Paris catering for live and inanimate targets.

The Company was also somewhat in advance of its time in producing a high quality catalogue in French. The school used the company's Swiftsure clay pigeon traps and many of these, both single and double rise versions were sold to fledgling sporting clay clubs in France.

Sales in Paris were excellent for over 20 years but by the 1930s the complicated tax systems and more particularly, fluctuations in the rate of exchange, made the continuation of the business unrealistic. The Paris business was sold to the manager of the Paris shop for the price of its goodwill and it continued along similar lines for a number of years.

In the 1950s the company's brochures stated that there were agents in Jamaica, South Africa, East Africa, West Africa, New Zealand, the USA, Canada, India, Pakistan, Australia, Ceylon, Egypt and France. Paris had the only Cogswell & Harrison shop outside England.

The first page of the French catalogue of 1909 which shows the Paris shop front.

COGSWELL & HARRISON Ltd.

MAISON FONDÉE EN 1770

Les plus grands fabricants à LONDRES de Fusils et Carabines de Chasse

MANUFACTURE D'ARMES : Gillingham St. près Victoria Station, LONDRES
FABRIQUE de MUNITIONS et POUDRES PYROXYLÉES : Colnbrook, près LONDRES
MAGASINS : LONDRES, 141, New Bond St. et 226, Strand
PARC DE TIR : Colnbrook, près LONDRES

COGSWELL & HARRISON Lᵈ·

ARMES

26, Avenue de l'Opéra ♣ PARIS

TÉLÉPHONE : 269-84

From the French catalogue of 1909.

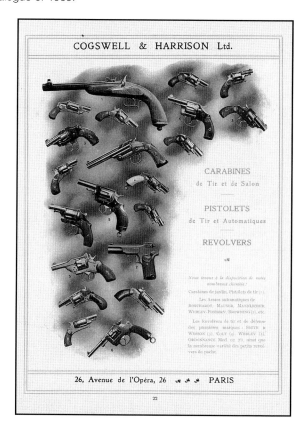

# 12  The Piccadilly Showrooms

The Piccadilly showrooms were opened in 1917 during the First World War and were manned by a very depleted staff. John E. Peskett who had left the company to serve in France with the Army Ordnance, returned from the war and was appointed Manager and trade picked up after 1918.

Major changes in Cogswell & Harrison took place after the war. Whilst the backbone of the company was at all times gunmaking, Piccadilly was also the location for many of the company's experiments in sporting goods diversification, at least some of which may in retrospect have been ill advised. It was decided to open up a fishing department so a manager with specialist experience in that field was recruited from Scotland and he engaged his own staff. High quality rods were made and new methods of gluing and setting were employed in the production of split cane rods that made them immensely strong and durable. Some of these rods still appear at auction.

Cogswell & Harrison were appointed sole agents for the Canadian firm of Pfluger and of Shakespeare who made steel rods and reels. Repair work was undertaken on rods and reels and dextrous female staff were employed to tie a special range of flies. The fishing department flourished for a time and was patronised by the Fly Fishers' Club.

As part of further expansion into related products an optical department was opened with its own dedicated manager. Equipment made by outside manufacturers such as Zeiss, Ross Barr and Stroud were sold and this area developed further with the company introducing its own range of field glasses made by a leading optical company.

Further developments included the opening of a Footwear Department and there was even a small dog department with everything required by the owners of gun dogs. Staff recall that John Peskett used to frequently say: "If only we had larger premises we could develop a department store".

The gun and field sports requirements of many famous patrons were provided by Cogswell & Harrison through the Piccadilly outlet. The shop was also a focal point for sportsmen and women from all over the world. Its location in Piccadilly made it highly desirable on a number of counts including some that were anecdotal. For example, Peskett recounts how in 1937 the showrooms were transformed for the coronation of George VI. The whole area of the showrooms was stripped of stock and showcases. Even the front windows were removed and seats installed to hold two hundred privileged spectators. Since entrance to the area was closed overnight, people had to take their seats the night before. In order to cater for their culinary needs, a running buffet was installed in the basement and 'much joviality ensued'.

168 Piccadilly was by far the best known of the Cogswell & Harrison premises. This is due partly to the fact that it functioned up to 1982 and partly because of the sheer volume of business carried out there. To this day there are thousands of sportsmen all over the world who fondly recall their visits to the shop. From 1928 when the Strand premises was sold, it was the only West End outlet for the company.

The diversification was tending to distract attention from the primary gunmaking business and had to be re-focussed. Furthermore, there was a depression in trade generally preceding the huge problems of the 1930s. Thus on 22 June 1932 an Extraordinary General Meeting at Andertons Hotel passed a resolution that the company should go into voluntary liquidation. This followed an order of the court that the whole of the property assets of Cogswell & Harrison had been secured to debenture holders. In 1932 a new limited company was formed under the direction of Edgar Harrison, John Peskett, Mr de Cordova and Mr Hazeldine. Fortunately for the company, it was possible to retain all the old skilled staff and administrative workers and as a result Cogswell & Harrison was soon functioning as previously.

In September 1939 on the declaration of the Second World War, the company again re-focussed its efforts and the nature of its output as part of the national war effort. Fortunately, the showroom sustained only slight and superficial damage throughout the blitz. However, the Acton factory was now the centre of activity as described earlier.

There was also a re-focussing of products in the Piccadilly showrooms to provide items required by civilians during the war. Torches were in great demand and Cogswell & Harrison responded with the manufacture of an 'indestructible' water-proof rubber torch. Contemporary reports stated that the company enjoyed 'a phenomenal trade in these items'. Other items popular with American servicemen were paper knives made from the shrapnel found in London streets after bombing raids; in some respects the showrooms assumed more the character of a hardware store.

Food supplies were very tight, so the control of vermin such as rabbit and pigeon was important in order to minimise the damage to crops and also to provide a useful source of additional food. To assist with the organised shoots for that purpose, special pest control cartridges were introduced. Furthermore, in dealing with pigeons, John Peskett invented a papier maché decoy pigeon that sold in thousands. To make these decoys durable in wet weather they were subsequently moulded in rubber and produced in a variety of patterns with annual sales exceeding ten thousand pieces. This laid the basis for a range of decoys including duck, geese, magpies and birds of prey. Cogswell & Harrison became a leading manufacturer of decoys in the post-war period.

In 1942, John Peskett applied for a patent for 'a testing device' that could be used on shotguns, rifles and pistols. It was of obvious military significance. It involved projecting a light beam on to the target when the trigger was pulled, thereby displaying the accuracy of the aim. In a modified form, it became a part of the company's gunfitting procedures and was used as a form of try-gun that was an additional refinement in gunfitting. The company reported: 'This device was used with great success in the Piccadilly showrooms for many years.'

Directly after the war there was a great demand for secondhand shotguns by those who had earlier surrendered their guns to the Ministry of Supply in a purchase arrangement. Cogswell & Harrison re-purchased large numbers of these and overhauled them. As a consequence, the Piccadilly shop made significant sales in these reconditioned guns and rifles and so the Piccadilly showrooms once again assumed their more traditional gun shop characteristics.

Cogswell & Harrison participated in the 1951 Festival of Britain by displaying newly produced guns and a particular attraction was the stand with craftsmen demonstrating their gunmaking skills in public. The demand for shotguns and rifles increased steadily and in the mid 1950s the company became known as the largest

John Peskett (right) selling a best gun at the Piccadilly showrooms.

The Piccadilly Showrooms, with Ted Holden on the right.

stockist in England of all the well known models of pistols and revolvers together with an impressive range of rifles. During this period, King Feisal of Iraq and King Hussein of Jordan were regular visitors to the Piccadilly shop.

The company's ever-recurring urge to diversify was evident. In 1957 an underwater fishing department was developed and Ted Holden, then a director of Cogswell & Harrison became a founder member of the British Sub Aqua Club. Also in 1957 Ted Holden saw the potential of hiring all types of arms and equipment to film making companies. Since such films would require not just British but also German, French and American props, a truly international effort was made to accumulate supplies which were the basis of a quite profitable business for a number of years.

Throughout this period the emphasis had shifted to the supply of surplus ex-Government rifles and equipment all of which had been reconditioned, re-proofed and tested at Acton. The result was a demand for increased space and developmental facilities. It was at this point that Sam Cummings, President of the International Armament Corporation of America and Canada, offered to purchase the ordinary shares of Cogswell & Harrison Ltd. The Board agreed and in December 1957 the transfer took place.

The Piccadilly shop remained the focal point during this period and in 1959, Sam Cummings took over a number of British companies so that, for example, Charles Boswell's address was given as 168 Piccadilly. The Cogswell & Harrison Rifle and Pistol Club was formed around this time with Stuart Murray as President. Vice Presidents were Ted Holden and Tom Littlewood. The directors presented a number of target rifles as prizes.

Advertisement for Decoys from *Shooting Times & Country Magazine*, 19 January 1967.

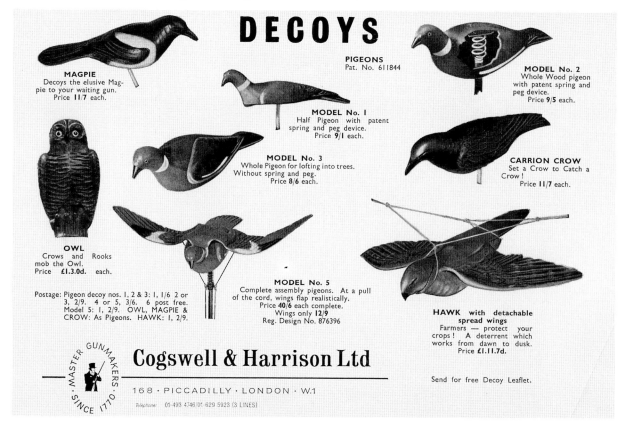

# DECOYS

**MAGPIE**
Decoys the elusive Magpie to your waiting gun.
Price 11/7 each.

**PIGEONS**
Pat. No. 611844

**MODEL No. 2**
Whole Wood pigeon with patent spring and peg device.
Price 9/5 each.

**MODEL No. 1**
Half Pigeon with patent spring and peg device.
Price 9/1 each.

**MODEL No. 3**
Whole Pigeon for lofting into trees. Without spring and peg.
Price 8/6 each.

**CARRION CROW**
Set a Crow to Catch a Crow!
Price 11/7 each.

**OWL**
Crows and Rooks mob the Owl.
Price £1.3.0d. each.

Postage: Pigeon decoy nos. 1, 2 & 3: 1, 1/6 2 or 3, 2/9. 4 or 5, 3/6. 6 post free. Model 5: 1, 2/9. OWL, MAGPIE & CROW: As Pigeons. HAWK: 1, 2/9.

**MODEL No. 5**
Complete assembly pigeons. At a pull of the cord, wings flap realistically.
Price 40/6 each complete.
Wings only 12/9
Reg. Design No. 876396

**HAWK with detachable spread wings**
Farmers — protect your crops! A deterrent which works from dawn to dusk.
Price £1.11.7d.

## Cogswell & Harrison Ltd

168 · PICCADILLY · LONDON · W.1
*Telephone:* 01-493 4746/01-629 5923 (3 LINES)

MASTER GUNMAKERS · SINCE 1770

Send for free Decoy Leaflet.

A well known figure in the Piccadilly Showrooms was Andrew Tucker, who was selected for the British team in 1962 to compete in the Dewar Hatch Cup against America and South Africa. In the intervening years he has won many honours and become a well-known personality at Bisley. Today he runs his own successful business in Cobham, Surrey.

Throughout this period the Piccadilly shop continued to be a 'must' for country sports people visiting London. When in March 1963 the retail business name and goodwill of Cogswell & Harrison was purchased from Sam Cummings by John Peskett and Ted Holden with other British shareholders, the Piccadilly showrooms continued as the showcase for the company's products. In 1970 it was the focal point of the Bicentenary celebrations and a banner head declaring this hung over the shop.

Throughout the 1970s it was extensively refitted to accommodate what may be seen in retrospect as somewhat erratic shifts in business emphasis. It was divided into a number of separate sections: there was a large section dealing with new and secondhand English guns; adjacent to this was a department for foreign side-by-side guns, automatic pump actions, over-and-unders and single barrel guns. It was also a period of rapid development in air rifle technology with an associated demand. To meet this the company opened a special department stating, 'our new air rifle department has probably one of the largest selections of target and sporting weapons in Great Britain'. To support this department, an air rifle target range was built on the lower ground floor facilitating the test firing of the air rifles on the premises. There was a revolver and pistol department that, as the company advertisement pointed out, had 'probably the most comprehensive range of pistols and revolvers available in the UK'.

The range of shooting-related products on offer was huge with a growing emphasis on foreign guns although the company also continued to produce fine shotguns of its own make. A new clothing department was opened with a comprehensive selection of shooting and outdoor clothing items. In addition to these departments, the company set up a special overseas department entitled 'Sport for Export'.

At that stage, Cogswell & Harrison had agents in many parts of the world. During this period the company referred to itself as Master Gunmakers of Piccadilly. Certainly the extensive and spacious layout of the showrooms attracted large numbers of customers. Many sportsmen working in London's banks, insurance companies and government departments used to throng to the showrooms and spend their lunch hours browsing amongst the latest offerings.

Like many older companies, Cogswell & Harrison had Memoranda of Association which were of a general and catch-all kind. In the case of Cogswell & Harrison they were in a form which allowed, indeed encouraged diversification and expansion.

## Mauser Broomhandle Pistol Cases

Many Cogswell & Harrison products became household names and the company made highly regarded specialist items for particular niche markets. The Swiftsure claypigeon trap is a case in point and was widely used around the turn of the century. In a similar vein the eye corrector was synonymous with the company's name for shooters with a dominant left eye.

Mauser broomhandle pistols had a dedicated following, with collectors and specialist clubs in many parts of the world. To set off their treasured pistols, the company offered a London handmade case. This was a high quality leather case fitted with either brass or leather corners, two straps and including six baize-lined compartments. These were block fitted to take the pistol, the wood holster/stock, the cleaning rod and the magazine clips. From the early 1900s they became the preferred case for many proud Mauser pistol owners. In fact one of the cases was featured (p 56) in *The Mauser Self Loading Pistol* by J.N. Belford and J. Dunlap.

This product was discontinued during the Second World War. More recently the company was encouraged to re-introduce the range by the specialist Mauser pistol company CRM International from whom they are available.

# Part Three: Sporting Guns and Ammunition

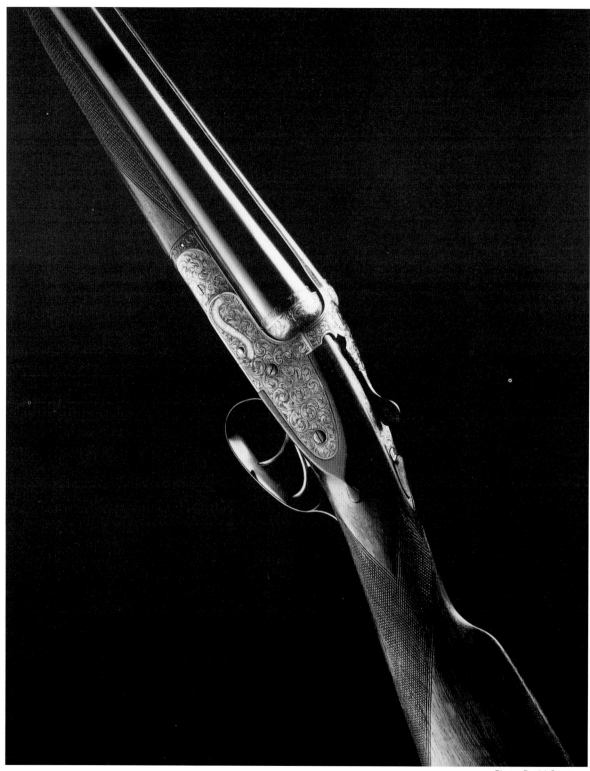

12-bore Ambassador No. 80,224. One of the models introduced to celebrate the company's bicentenary.
(C. Hallatt collection).

# 13  The Ingenious Harrisons

Patents are granted to individuals and companies who can lay claim to a new product, manufacturing process or an improvement to an existing product or process which was not previously known in the United Kingdom or elsewhere. The granting of a patent gives the patentee a monopoly to make, use or sell the invention for a fixed period of time (currently 20 years from when the application was first filed). The earliest known English patent was granted in 1449 and prior to 1852, when the patent system was overhauled by the Patent Law Amendment Act, the process was haphazard and prone to abuse. Before 1852 protection within the law was provided by registration with the Designs Registry. This was set up in 1839 to protect the designs of manufactured articles and became the responsibility of the Patent Office in 1875.

When confronted with a mechanical problem, a group of skilled artisans will offer nearly as many solutions as there are individuals. Although each solution may outwardly appear to be different, there will often be a common theme running through them all. So in addition to giving an insight into the workings of an inventive mind, a close examination of patents granted can reveal much about the evolution of a technology and how an individual, working alone or in conjunction with others contributed to its development.

Patents reveal that inventing is not always limited to single ideas isolated in time but often represents a process of parallel evolution, where each invention is one individual's contribution to the solution of a much larger problem.

Nowhere is this more true than in the inventions of Edward and Edgar Harrison and their collaborators. A search of the patent abridgements at the London Patent Office reveals that, during the period 1864 to 1929, Edward and Edgar Harrison either individually, jointly or in collaboration with others filed 24 patent applications of which 17 were granted and seven abandoned. The applications cover not only shotgun mechanisms but also gunsights, cartridge loading machines, pistol and rifle mechanisms and air weapons.

Of the patents which are concerned solely with shotgun mechanisms there are significant contributions to the fields of cocking mechanisms (both pinfire and hammerless centre-fire ones), safety mechanisms, ejectors and a single trigger mechanism.

Shotgun Patents:

| | | | |
|---|---|---|---|
| 271 | (1864) | Edward Harrison | Cocking Mechanism |
| 278 | (1880) | Edward Harrison & Thomas Southgate | Cocking Mechanism |
| 1,903 | (1883) | Edward Harrison & Frederick Beesley | Cocking Mechanism |
| 15,272 | (1886) | Edgar Harrison | Cocking Mechanism |
| 16,214 | (1886) | Edgar Harrison | Cocking Mechanism |
| 14,444 | (1887) | Edgar Harrison & Edwin Anson | Cocking Mechanism |
| 18,157 | (1888) | Edgar Harrison | Cocking & Ejector Mechanism |
| 11,550 | (1888) | Edgar Harrison | Ejector Mechanism |
| 18,157 | (1888) | Edgar Harrison | Cocking & Ejector Mechanism |

| 13,591 | (1889) | Edgar Harrison | Ejector Mechanism |
|---|---|---|---|
| 20,234 | (1890) | Edgar Harrison | Ejector Mechanism |
| 4,005 | (1895) | Edgar Harrison | Single Trigger |

Other Patents:

| 1,326 | (1886) | Edgar Harrison & William Jeffery | Gun sights |
|---|---|---|---|
| 7,029 | (1886) | Edgar Harrison & William Jeffery | Gun sights |
| 4,097 | (1900) | Edgar Harrison | Bolt action rifle |
| 13,382 | (1901) | Edgar Harrison & Joseph Bonel | Recoil operated firearms |
| 330,105 | (1929) | Edgar Harrison | Air Pistols |

Many of the famous names in English gunmaking, Thomas Southgate, Frederick Beesley, William Jeffery and Edwin Anson were collaborators. Edwin was the son of William Anson who with John Deeley is credited with one of the most significant developments in English gunmaking, patent No. 1,756 of 1875, for what we today refer to as the Anson & Deeley boxlock action.

The earliest recorded patent is No. 271 of 1 February 1864 which describes Edward Harrison's self half-cocking pinfire mechanism and single rotating bolt snap action. Harrison's action has an underlever, which curves around the trigger guard and rotates on a transverse pivot at the bottom of the action, below and slightly forward of the face. The head of the underlever, a rounded hook facing forwards, engages with a rear-facing hook on the lump of the barrels. When pushed forward and down, the head of the lever releases the hook on the barrel lump and presses against the underside of the lump, causing the breech end of the barrels to be raised off the face of the action.

Simultaneously a swivel link attached to the rear part of the head of the underlever moves downwards. Connected to this link is a lifter, working on a pivot fixed in a lug formed on the back part of the action body. The front end of the lifter is forked and each fork passes through

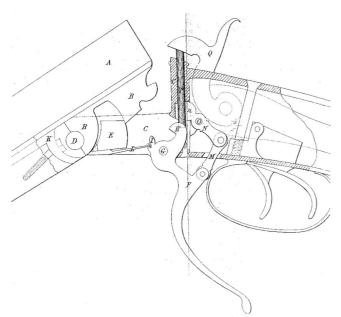

Patent No. 271 of 1864.

a slot in a pair of lifting pins. The lifting pins rise and fall, in cylindrical cavities in the action body immediately below the hammers. So, as the underlever is pushed forwards and down, the breech end of the barrels rises and levers lift the hammers clear of the pins and half cock the locks.

On closing the gun the hook on the barrel lump bears down on the hook on the head of the underlever forcing the lever back. A leaf spring under the bar of the action and fixed at its forward end, bears down on a forward facing projection on the head of the underlever forward of the pivot, holding the lever in the shut position.

A 16-year gap exists before we see the next of Edward Harrison's patents. This is No. 278 of 22 January 1880 in which he collaborates with Thomas Southgate on a

Plate 7  An Extra Quality Victor 12-bore BLE with ornamental sideplates, Avant Tout ejectors and assisted opening mechanism. No. 27,251, it was completed in May 1901. *(Courtesy Dr Killidar.)*

A pin-fire 12-bore double rifle, No. 5,982 with automatic half-cocking mechanism. It had one standard sight and two leaf sights to 200 yards. *( R. Sykes Collection.)*

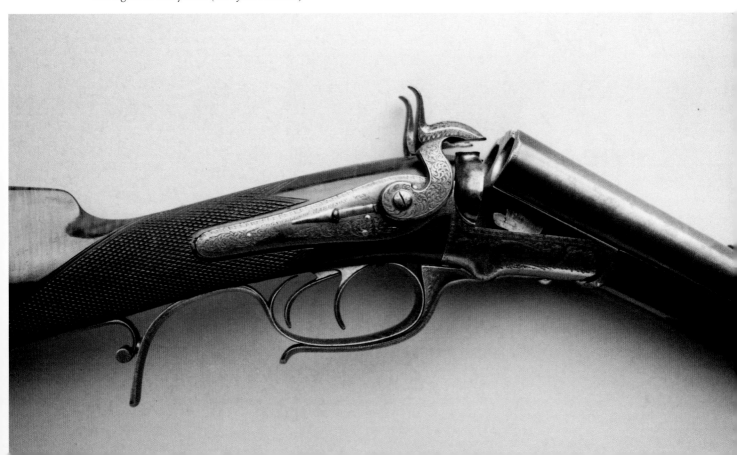

Plate 8

A Grand Prix Pigeon gun, No. 40,521, completed in 1906 on a BLE action with ornamental sideplates. Models ranged from simple BLEs to the high quality Victor SLEs.

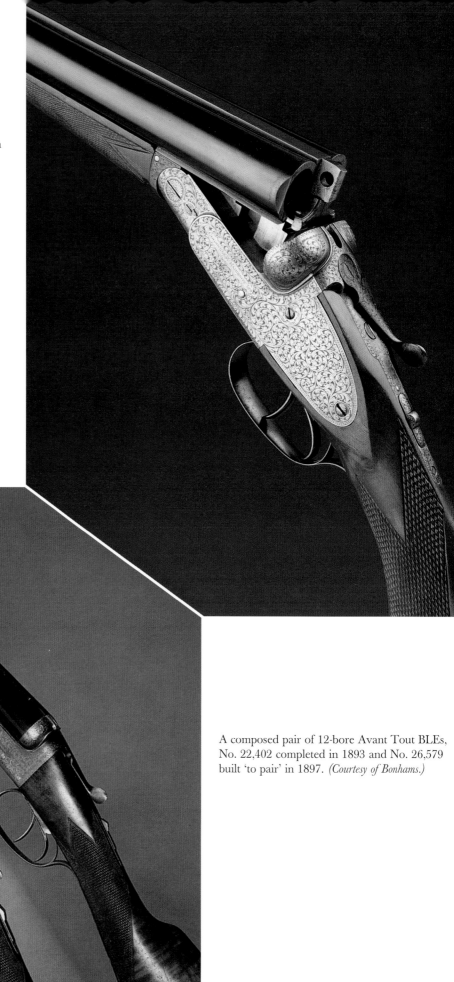

A composed pair of 12-bore Avant Tout BLEs, No. 22,402 completed in 1893 and No. 26,579 built 'to pair' in 1897. *(Courtesy of Bonhams.)*

Plate 9

A 12-bore Cosmos Ball and Shot gun, No. 42,975, completed on 23 September 1908. The Cosmos was available in 8-, 10-, 12-, 16- or 20-bore in SLE or BLE models.
*(Cogswell & Harrison collection.)*

(below) A pair of Huntic side-lock ejectors, Nos 57,488/57,650, built in 1937. The 27½ in. barrels weigh 2 lb 14 oz. Each gun was 6 lb 7 oz.
*(Courtesy A. Cleave.)*

Plate 10  A matched pair of Victor sidelock ejectors also shown on the front cover, Nos 44,979/44,980, built in 1912. *(Courtesy J. Baert.)*

self-cocking snap action. Thomas Southgate is best known for his ejector mechanism patented in 1893 and often referred to as the Holland & Holland type. The Southgate ejector is probably the simplest and most popular of all ejector mechanisms. It has only two moving parts (a kicker and spring), is fully selective, only operates if the gun has been fired and is housed in the forend.

Harrison and Southgate's invention received only provisional protection and unfortunately, the specification contains no illustrations. It describes a mechanism where a side lever is used to open a gun, withdrawing the locking bolts. When used on a single-barrel gun it also cocks the action. When used in a double-barrel gun the opening of the action and the lowering of the barrels cock the action. In addition to the cocking mechanism, Harrison and Southgate claim a novel kind of knuckle joint which enables the barrels to be detached without having to remove the forend. Also they describe gas-tight strikers and a self-acting safety to prevent accidental discharge.

Edward Harrison's next patent was also a collaboration, this time with one of the most respected names in English gunmaking, Frederick Beesley, who was a prolific inventor. Indeed it was said that his unofficial title was 'Inventor to the London Gun Trade' and other makers used many of his inventions. Beesley was apprenticed in 1861 aged 15 to the firm of Moore & Grey in Old Bond Street, later to become William Moore & Grey who were eventually purchased by Cogswell & Harrison in 1908. He subsequently worked his way through the London gun trade before finding himself at James Purdey where he worked on the design that was to become the famous Purdey action, before setting up business on his own at 22 Queen Street, Edgware Road in 1879. Beesley's self-opening hammerless action incorporated a mechanism by which the mainsprings were compressed when the gun was closed.

The mechanism was protected by Patent No. 31 of 3 January 1880. On 29 July of the same year Beesley agreed to assign the patent to James Purdey subject to a payment of £20 and royalties of 5 shillings per gun until 'the number of Guns made by James Purdey, or his Agent or Agents, shall have amounted to Two Hundred, whereupon such Royalty shall cease'. James Purdey astutely retained the right to commute the royalty of 5 shillings per gun on the payment of £35. This he did and on 16 November 1880 Frederick Beesley signed for receipt of James Purdey's cheque for £35, which gave Purdey complete control of the Beesley action and protection for fourteen years.

Patent No. 1,903 of 1883, left-hand lock

Harrison and Beesley's Patent No. 1,903 of 14 April 1883, is concerned with a barrel-cocking mechanism which the inventors claim is '. . . enabled to use the power developed in the actions both of opening and closing the gun for the purpose of cocking either lock by either of those actions desired'. The illustrations in the patent show the left lock being cocked on opening the gun and the right lock being cocked as the gun is closed.

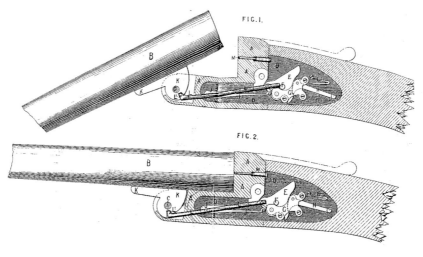

The idea is a basic one and principal parts of the mechanism are common to both modes of operation. Both locks have a cocking lever pivoted on the front of the action bar and share a common centre with the barrels. The left lock is cocked by a sliding rod pushed against the breast of the hammer by a notch cut into the lower part of a cam fitted to the underside of the barrels where they pivot. The cam rotates upwards when the gun is opened and when the gun is closed the cam engages the front end of the cocking rod and draws it back out of the way of the hammer so not to block its fall. The right lock is cocked as the gun is closed by a notch cut into a cam above the barrel pivot similarly engaging a cocking rod, which acts against the right hammer.

In order to prevent the right cocking rod from blocking the fall of the hammer when the gun is discharged, the rear of the cocking rod is hinged and made to slide over the cocking stud on the hammer as the rod reaches the extent of its rearward travel. When the barrels are opened the cam moves round engaging the front end of the cocking rod drawing it forward and a spring fitted to the hinged end of the rod drops it back into position ready to push against the cocking stud.

The patent abridgements list the next patent application No. 7,437 of 8 May 1884 as that of E. & E. Harrison in connection with self-cocking break-down firearms. Here it would appear that we have the only collaboration between Edward and Edgar Harrison. Unfortunately the application was abandoned and no records of the actual specification exist.

Next in chronological order we have patent No. 11,382 of 18 August 1884 for an intercepting block safety mechanism. Again it is a collaboration and again we have Frederick Beesley as co-inventor but on this occasion it is with Edgar Harrison, whose address is given as 142 New Bond Street. Safeties such as these, where the tumblers are restrained by a lever mechanism which is automatically released by pulling the trigger, were widely applied to 'best-quality' guns and remain in common usage in one variety or another.

Harrison and Beesley's solution was accomplished by fixing a lever to the trigger plate where the front end blocks the action of the lock mechanism (either the mainspring or the tumbler) and the rear end is activated by a trigger via a small projection on the lever passing through a hole cut in the upper part of the trigger blade. The complete specification is brief, containing only 45 lines of text of which almost ten lines are Harrison and Beesley's addresses and the declaration of the nature of the invention.

In the next two patents, No. 1,326 of 29 January 1886 and No. 7,029 of 25 May 1886, we have Edgar Harrison who is now giving his address as 226 The Strand, collaborating with William J. Jeffery of 23 Whiteheads Grove, Chelsea. William Jackman Jeffery was born in 1857 and first appears as an inventor in 1885 with his patent No. 12,345 for a mirror 'bore inspector' for the internal inspection of gun barrels. He gives his address as 42 Great Castle Street which, in contemporary records, was listed as being occupied by a Corn Merchant not a gunmaker.

On his next patent of 1886 in collaboration with Edgar Harrison, he states his occupation as Gunmaker's Salesman. There is speculation that he might have been working for Cogswell & Harrison at the time but there is no corroborating evidence. Following this, William Jeffery was briefly the manager of P. Webley & Son's London premises before setting up in business first as Jeffery & Davies and finally as W. J. Jeffery & Co. The company will be best remembered for its double rifles, many in large calibres, and for its range of rifle cartridges.

The patents for vernier rifle sights, windgauges and foresight protectors, are an early indication of Edgar Harrison's general interest in firearms and his willingness to diversify beyond shotgun mechanisms. If Edgar Harrison's last collaboration with Fredrick Beesley yielded a short specification, his collaborations with William Jeffery are nothing if not concise. Patent No. 1,326 contains only 35 lines of text including names, addresses and the description of the illustration whilst No. 7,029 manages to contain everything within 25 lines of text.

The brevity with which these two inventions are described is a reflection of their simplicity. The first describes a design for a rifle rearsight to enable accurate wind allowance to be made and the adjustments recorded from the vernier gauge. The second patent describes a one-piece drawn metal shield for covering the foresight of military and other rifles.

Edgar Harrison's next patent application, No. 13,839 of 28 October 1886 described a means of 'Ejecting cartridges from breech-loading firearms' It was abandoned and no details remain other than the title.

The next complete patent specification is No. 15,272 of 23 November 1886 which is another cocking mechanism, although Harrison describes it grandly as being 'to enable the barrels and fore part of hammerless sporting fire-

Patent No. 15,272 of 1886.

arms to be placed on and off the stock when locks are in uncocked position, and to reduce friction'. This he achieved by using a cam pivoted on the forward end of the cocking lever, which bears on the underside of the barrels in front of the hinge pin. The cam is held in position by a cross-piece fitted to the forend iron. This arrangement allows both the barrels and forend to be taken off the action when the locks are in the uncocked (fired) position.

If Edgar Harrison's earlier collaboration with William Jeffery produced a concise specification, his patent No. 16,214 of 10 December 1886 lies at the other extreme. Interestingly, this patent was amended on 29 November 1888 under Sections 18 to 21 of the 1883 Patents, Designs and Trademarks Act. These amendments added another four pages to the already lengthy text and 35 figures.

The patent is concerned with both opening cocking and ejector mechanisms for drop down guns. Cocking of the lockwork is achieved using a series of levers and

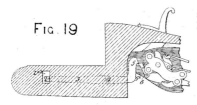

Patent No. 16,214 of 1886.

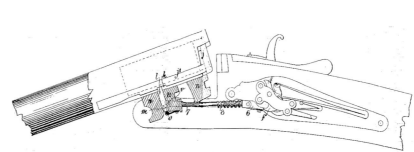

rods acted on by a collar fitted around the hinge pin, which rotates as the gun is opened and the barrels pivot downwards. A short rod hinged to the collar moves backwards as the collar rotates. The rear end of the rod is hinged to another vertical lever pivoted at its bottom end near the floor of the action. The movement of the top of this vertical lever is greater than the movement of the rod from the collar and this greater movement is transmitted by another lever to the breast of the tumbler. So via two horizontal rods and one vertical lever the opening of the barrels cocks the gun.

Harrison also included an ejector mechanism by which the cocking lever is used as an ejector trip. To trip the ejector the third lever, which acts against the breast of the tumbler, is continued forward and has an upward projection at its forward end. When the gun has been fired this upward projection engages with the stem of the ejector. The stem is restrained until the projection slips out when the barrels have opened enough for the empty cases to clear the breach. In many ways this patent is the forerunner to modern ejectors in that the system described has a separate mechanism for each barrel.

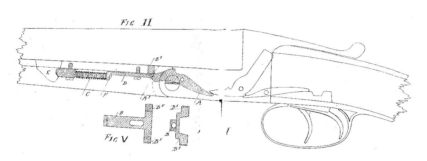

Patent No.14,444 of 1887.

1887 was a less productive year for Edgar Harrison: he only produced one successful patent application, Patent No. 14,444 of 24 October, in which he collaborated with Edwin George Anson on a cocking mechanism for drop down guns. Edwin was the son of William Anson who with John Deeley is credited with one of the most significant developments in English gunmaking, Patent No. 1, 756 of 1875, for what we today refer to as the Anson & Deeley boxlock action.

Edwin followed his father into the gun trade and completed his first patent application, No. 12,402 for an ejector mechanism, the year before his collaboration with Edgar Harrison. Interestingly Edwin's father William patented an ejector mechanism later the same year (No. 16,318 in 1886). Harrison and Anson's mechanism uses cocking lifters pivoted behind the cross pin and activated by a slide in the forend. The slide is held in position against the cocking lifters by a spring which in one version of the mechanism also holds the forend iron in place against the barrel loop. The rear facing ends of the cocking lifters simply engage with the bottom of the tumblers on opening the gun and force the tumblers into the cocked position.

Mentioned in the title 'An Improved Method of Cocking and Making Safe Hammerless Guns and Rifles' is a safety mechanism in provisional specification only. In slots at the backs of the tumblers are catches operated by springs. These engage with the sears when the gun is opened. Lifters worked by the triggers lift the tumbler catches away from the sears allowing the tumblers to fall when the gun is fired.

Harrison was inactive in the field of patenting until the following year when on 10 February 1888 he made application No. 2,027 in collaboration with a D. Gibson for a cartridge loading machine which was abandoned, leaving no record other than the inclusion in the patent abridgements. His next attempt was more successful and

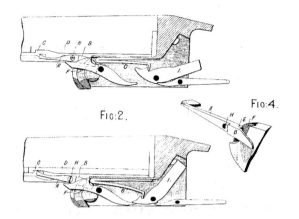

Fig:2.

Fig:4.

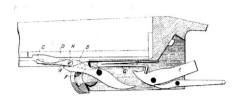

Patent No. 11,550 of 1888.

patent application No. 11,550 of 10 August 1888 for an ejector mechanism for drop
down guns was incorporated into one of Cogswell & Harrison's most successful
designs, the Avant Tout action.

The company used the Avant Tout hammerless ejector action as the basis for a
number of guns. The company's 1908 catalogue lists four of them. Edgar Harrison's
invention harnesses the forward motion of the mainspring of an Anson & Deeley
boxlock action to trip the ejector mechanism. This is done by allowing the forward
end of the mainspring to slide over the rear of the ejector sear allowing it to engage
with the extractor. The ejector then trips as the gun is opened as the rear end of the
ejector sear bears on a shoulder on the knuckle of the action.

Later the same year Edgar Harrison produced yet another patent
application describing an ejector mechanism. In patent No. 18,157 of
12 December 1888 he describes a means of simultaneously compressing the mainspring and ejecting the spent cartridge in drop
down guns. He bases his mechanism on using the upward motion of
the cocking lever to lift the ejector sears into engagement with the
ejector leg. To do this he employs a lever pivoted in the fore end,
whose forward end engages in a notch cut in the ejector leg and the
rear part of which is acted on by the cocking lever.

When the gun is opened, the cocking lever is pressed forward
against the rear of the ejector sear, forcing its forward end into the
notch in the ejector leg, where it becomes locked in position where
it can press against the cocking lever, thus compressing the mainspring. As soon as
the tumblers are cocked, the ejector sear is rotated about its pivot bringing its
forward end out of the notch in the ejector leg thus releasing it to eject the spent
cartridge.

When the gun is opened while still cocked, the pressure of the tumbler is removed
from the cocking mechanism and the forward end of the ejector sear is kept down
by a leaf spring, so the ejector leg extracts but does not eject the unfired cartridge.
The complete specification illustrates the mechanism as applied to both boxlock and
sidelock actions.

Harrison also shows his invention combined with and applied to Thomas Perkes'
action described in Patent No. 1,968 of 1878. Perkes' invention is regarded by many
as one of the most important British shotgun patents in that it uses a cocking rod

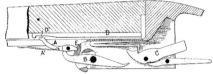

Fig:2.

Patent No. 18,157 of
1888.

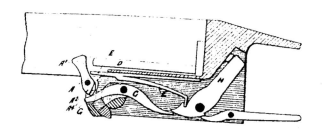

Patent No. 13,591 of 1889.

running from the action knuckle to the breast of the tumbler to cock the action when the barrels pivot open. Harrison also shows it applied to his earlier patent No.16,214 of 1886.

Edgar Harrison's next patent, No.13, 591 of 28 August 1889, was a main spring powered ejector mechanism or to quote Harrison, a mechanism to '…simplify the construction and action of the ejector mechanism'. It uses an ejector tumbler whose rear end is pressed downwards by the bottom of the cocking lever when the gun pivots open. This causes the front of the ejector tumbler to act on a cam in the forend. As the gun is opened, the cam moves backwards until it reaches a point where the pressure from the cocking lever (transmitted via the ejector tumbler) moves forward of the pivot point of the ejector tumbler which is flicked back against the ejector leg.

His next patent application, No. 6,723 of 1 May 1890, described simply as 'Stocks for Firearms', was abandoned and as such no details remain other than the title. The next successful application was another ejector mechanism, No. 20,234 of 11 December 1890 titled 'Improvements in Ejecting Mechanism for Drop Down Sporting Fire-arms'.

This fourth and final ejector mechanism patent concerns itself with two methods of tripping the ejectors and makes reference to his earlier patent No. 16,214 of 1886. One mechanism describes an ejector tripping rod having a pivoted catch fitted to its rear end. This catch engages with a projection on the underside of the tumbler, which when being re-cocked pushes the ejector tripping rod forward and in doing so trips the ejector mechanism.

Harrison does not take the trouble to describe a specific ejector mechanism. Instead he makes reference to his earlier patent and the mechanisms described therein. Harrison then goes on to describe the use of the back-and-forth rocking motion of a sidelock mainspring to trip the ejector mechanism. He achieves this by using the

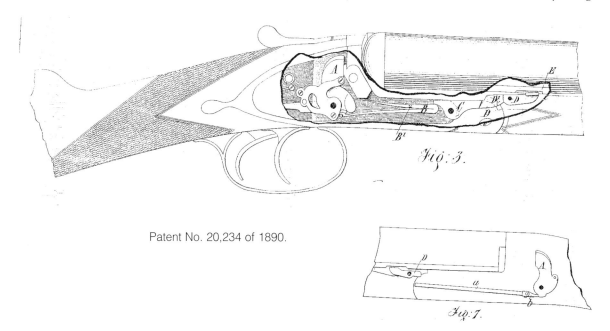

Patent No. 20,234 of 1890.

upward motion of the front of the mainspring to raise the rear of a lever set in the knuckle of the action which, when depressed, forces down a sear in the forend allowing it to engage with the ejector stem. So when the gun is opened, the rear end of the sear is acted on by a projection on the knuckle and the ejectors are tripped to expel the fired case or cases.

In his next patent, No. 4,005 of 25 February 1895, Edgar Harrison provided the detailed specification of one of the first effective single selective trigger mechanisms. In his design a tumbler, or elevating lever is fitted at the rear of an ordinary shaped trigger, the upper end of which may be in two positions: first, under the right sear; second, under the left sear. In firing the first barrel of the gun the trigger is pulled and during its upward travel comes against a stop which has the effect of turning the lever 90 degrees about its centre until it comes against another stop which may be the left sear. When the trigger returns to its rest position the elevating lever turns still further about its centre until its upper end is in the second position. When pulling the trigger to fire the left barrel, the lower rear end of the elevating lever comes against a second stop and performs the same function as above but in the opposite direction. When the gun is opened the trigger safety slide moves against the upper part of the elevating lever and places it in the first position. The mechanism is selective, allowing the firing sequence to be changed by means of a sliding lever, operated by a button on the rear of the trigger plate, which moves the elevating lever from one position to the other.

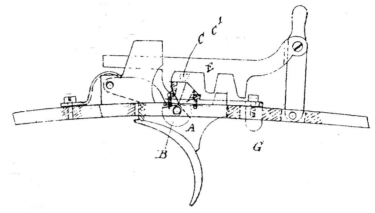

Patent No. 4,005 of 1895.

It is interesting to put Harrison's design in context with the development of the single trigger mechanism. Some of the earliest patented designs were those of John Robertson, the Proprietor of Boss & Co., starting with patent No. 20,873 of 3 November 1893, followed by No. 5,897 on 21 March 1894 and No. 22,894 on 26 November the same year. The Boss mechanism is based on a vertical drum containing a coil spring. On the first pull of the trigger a stop on the drum arrests the trigger blade until it is released by the second involuntary pull so that the trigger blade is lifted over the stop and moved across to engage the other sear.

Robertson's design is still regarded by many as the finest single trigger mechanism ever made. Robertson's patent however was not the earliest: that honour appears to belong to Patent No. 21,204 of 4 December 1891 in the name of A. A. Cook and W. Moore Grey. Harrison's patent was one of three in 1895 describing single trigger mechanisms: the others were H.A.A. Thorn, the proprietor of Lancaster, with No. 5,517 of 15 March and Fredrick Beesley's No. 10,133 of 22 May. Interestingly, both Thorn and Beesley's patents rely on the involuntary pull of the trigger finger to engage the trigger blade with the second sear.

Edgar Harrison's single trigger mechanism was his last successful shotgun patent. Following No. 4,005 there were three more applications, all of which were abandoned, leaving only the tantalisingly brief titles contained in the Patent Abridgements: No. 4,413 of 1 March 1895 'Small Arms'; No. 1,732 of 22 January

1898 'Small Arms' and No. 9,009 of 19 April 1898 'Firearms'. There was however a successful application in No. 24, 173 also of 22 January 1898, for Cycle Brakes which reflects the diversity of Harrison's interests.

The next successful firearms patent was No. 4,097 of 1 March 1900 for 'Improvements in Rifles' in which Harrison describes a bolt-action centre fire rifle mechanism. The patent claims almost the entire workings of a rifle including the means of securing the barrel, a sliding breech block, an ejector mechanism, a method of securing the bolt head to the breech, a safety mechanism and a rear sight. The following description from the company's catalogue quotes the Editor of *Land and Water* as clearly describing the working of the mechanism which, although a bolt-action differs from the Mauser type action developed in 1867 whilst retaining similarities to the Mannlicher-Schoenauer action:

> The rifle action is not one that can be likened to that of any existing weapon, military or otherwise upon the market. While possessed of a bolt, it is not the ordinary turn-bolt action.
>
> …it has been necessary to provide for a strong breech closure capable of resisting heavy recoil. To effect this purpose, the bolt fastenings are solid with the barrel. The bolt handle is situated immediately to the rear of the barrel, and is the foremost part of the sliding bolt. The bolt handle forms part of the bolt-head, which is the part locking into the barrel, and so closing the breech. It does this by means of lugs or side extensions, which obtain their grip by a quarter-turn of the bolt handle, the same as in ordinary bolt rifles, and analogous in action to the bayonet clutch. The remainder of the bolt, which is situated to the rear of the bolt-head and handle, is merely an appendage for the purpose of guiding the bolt in its reciprocating movements and effecting the minor operations of extracting and reloading. The removal of the bolt is a simple operation.

This sliding breech block was removed in the conventional manner by pressing the trigger and withdrawing the block while the barrel could also be detached by releasing a retaining screw and giving a half turn. In bolt-action weapons of the Mauser type the loading cycle involves the lifting of the bolt handle and drawing the bolt to the rear to expose the breech end of the barrel. On closing the bolt by pushing it forward the cartridge is positively locked in the breech by a camming action. The closed and locked mechanism can withstand high chamber pressures and, as such, bolt-actions can be built in heavy calibres.

The Mannlicher-Schoenauer design differs in that the bolt is operated by a straight backwards and forwards movement with no turning of the bolt being necessary so

Patent No. 4,097 of 1900.

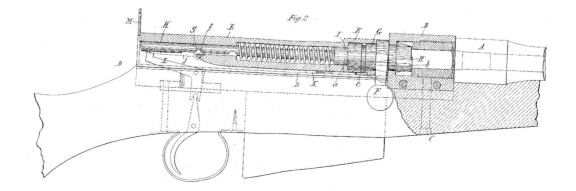

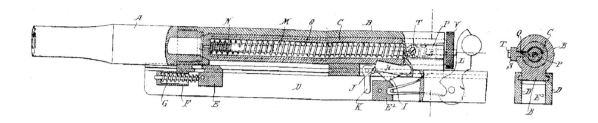

the bolt handle is drawn back through a bridge at the rear of the action to expose the magazine and breech. In Harrison's design the turning of the bolt handle is limited to a quarter turn. Cogswell & Harrison marketed the design under the name 'Certus' in a number of formats; a centre fire magazine rifle in ·400 calibre, a single shot rook rifle chambered for ·295 and ·250 calibre centre fire and as a marksman's rifle in ·22 rimfire.

Patent No. 13,382 of 1901.

In the his next patent, No. 13,382 of 1 July 1901, Harrison collaborated with Joseph Bonel, a worker at the company's Gillingham Street factory, on a simplified mechanism for the locking of the bolt in recoil operated firearms. Harrison and Bonel describe each moving part of the mechanism before simply claiming a mechanism for a recoiling breech block, a means for a limited movement of the barrel under recoil to unlock the bolt, extend movement of the bolt to eject the spent cartridge, load a fresh round and cock the hammer. The description is simply a recoil-operated, locked breech mechanism relying on the rearward movement of the barrel to impart sufficient energy to the breech mechanism to allow it eject the fired cartridge, reload and re-cock the hammer.

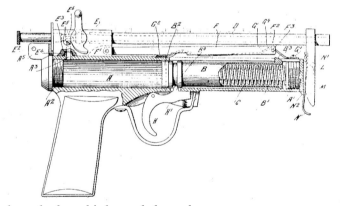

Edgar Harrison's final successful patent application was for Patent No. 330,105 of 9 May 1929 for 'Improvements in Air Pistols' and was granted only nine years before his death. Harrison is here seeking protection for more than mere improvements to an existing design. His patent covers the entire workings and mechanism for a spring-powered air pistol where the barrel is located above the air chamber and the spring compressed by elevating the hinged barrel. At first sight the illustrations in the patent are very similar to the familiar Webley air pistols. The Company's 1929 catalogue lists the design as the 'Certus' Air Pistol, which was available with a detachable stock for 40 shillings.

Patent No. 330,105 of 1929.

Edgar Harrison's ingenuity was not limited to gunmaking but extended to a range of scientific equipment and testing devices which he developed and used in the manufacture of firearms and the loading of cartridges. The book *Shooting: With Game and Gun-room Notes* by 'Blagdon' published by the company in 1900, describes a cap tester developed by Cogswell & Harrison for testing the composition of primer compounds and their crusher gauge.

The instrument was a gun barrel with a breech and firing mechanism fitted to one end and movable plugs fitted along its length at regular intervals; 1, 2½, 5½ in. etc.

A lead cylinder is placed on the head of each plug and the cylinder is crushed by the expanding gasses generated on ignition of the cartridge – the greater the strain the greater the compression. The cylinders are measured and compared to a table to convert the results into tons per square inch. The Editor of *The Field* for 6 May 1893 wrote:

> In no branch of sport has the aid of science been called in to a greater extent than in conjunction with shooting, and the instruments which have been employed and the experiments which have been made of recent years could never have been dreamed of by the old school of shooting men. To go no further than the invention of the new powders, a life of observation would be necessary to test their respective merits had they to be decided by the gun alone; but by employing a crusher gauge, a representation of which is given herewith, much valuable information is obtained in a single day. Crusher gauges, as our readers are no doubt aware, are instruments used for ascertaining the pressures given by gunpowder exploded in the barrel of a gun.
>     . . . Messers. Cogswell and Harrison have for many years used crusher gauges, acting on precisely the same principle as here set forth, and they invariably test nitro-powder supplied to them. To this fact, no doubt, much of the success which has been attended their cartridge-loading business must be attributed.

In *Experts on Guns and Shooting*, G. T. Teasdale-Buckell the editor of *Land and Water* from 1885 to 1889, gives an idea of Edgar Harrison's efforts to maintain a procedure for the quality control of bought-in powder:

> We suspect that most gunmakers now take the pressures of each new batch of nitro-powder that comes in, but it was, we think, Mr. Harrison who first did this, and thereby built up an enormous business as a retailer of loaded cartridges at prices ranging from £3 15s to £5 10s a thousand. We are not even now sure that many gunmakers take the trouble, not only to test internal pressures of new batches of powders, but also try velocities given by them. This Cogswell and Harrison do, and not only that, they test each new batch of primers also, so as to accommodate primers to powders or powders to primers, for it is well known that a slight variation in either makes a great difference to the manner of combustion of the charge, and therefore also greatly affects not only pressure on the barrels and velocity of shot, but time between the pull of the trigger and the starting of the shot.
>     . . . The gunmaker cannot control the weather, but he can, and should, test his powders for variation with the weather, and discard those whose ignition is delayed by damp. All this requires the chronograph to test, as well as the crusher-gauge, and these instruments Messers Cogswell and Harrison have long possessed, and used upon every batch of powder delivered to them, a fact which has sometimes brought them into sharp collision with the powder-makers. Mr. Harrison is now making half-a-dozen of Smith's chronographs for various powder manufacturers.

In his book *A Dissertation on Guns and Shooting* published in 1906, Harrison illustrates a number of instruments used in the manufacture of shotguns and rifles. These include the crusher gauge. For the testing of finished cartridges the company used a device which measured the force required to pull the top wad away from the turnover. For barrel making Cogswell & Harrison made extensive use of micrometer gauges for measuring barrel wall thickness in addition to manufacturing its own barrel, plug and rim gauges.

The last quarter of the nineteenth century was a period of tremendous technological innovation in British society. The term 'continuous innovation' now coined by some management gurus, could appropriately describe large sections of British society as the century drew to its close. The period was one of feverish activity in the gun trade where change and innovation were evident in abundance and Cogswell & Harrison were no exception. The company was steeped in this inventive tradition: from Edward Harrison's early developments through to Edgar Harrison's prolific inventions, the Harrisons successfully sought protection for seventeen patents, of which fourteen were in the short 20 year period from 1880 – 1900.

The Harrisons' extraordinary wide range of competencies and abilities manifested themselves throughout the company's golden years. This tradition of invention and innovation was only tempered by the death of Edgar Harrison in 1938.

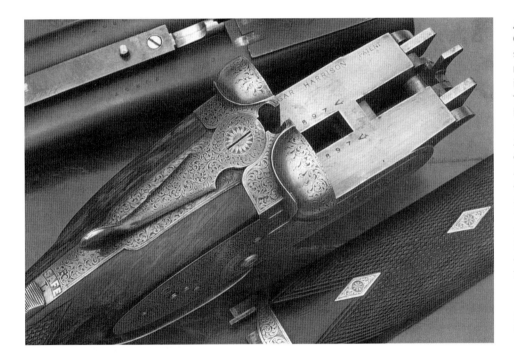

Although most Cogswell & Harrison single triggers were non-selective, some interesting exceptions were made based on customer preference. No. 20,897 was completed on 26 August 1892. The central position of the safety selector was 'SAFE' and the barrel selection was made by shifting it forwards or backwards from that central position.

(Courtesy of Sherman Bell and *Double Gun Journal*).

# 14  Shotguns

During the hundred years between 1870 and the company's bicentenary in 1970, Cogswell & Harrison introduced over twenty models of double-barrel side-by-side shotgun plus two over-and-unders and an assortment of single barrel guns. In retrospect the wisdom of such diversity may be questioned. Each shotgun was given a model name such as Victor, Crown and Tower but to add to the confusion, type numbers also identified the different models in some of the company records. To give just two examples, Type T110 referred to the Extra Quality Victor sidelock ejector and T206 to the side-plated boxlock named the Sandhurst. Thus, the owner of a sidelock may know that his gun is, for example, a Huntic model but may have little idea of where this gun fits into the Cogswell & Harrison price range. In some cases models were of the same basic technical specification but were of different grades depending on the extent of embellishment and, for example, the quality of walnut selected for the stock.

In the case of a boxlock there were also different models and grades. In one model range the guns were all fitted with Avant Tout ejectors and assisted opening mechanism. The grades were identified in three ways: by a model name, by a letter (for example, there was the 'P' quality Avant Tout, the 'S' quality, the 'N' quality and so on) and in some records by a type number as well. The eight grades of boxlock in the early 1900s were headed by the 'X' quality, known as the Extra Quality Victor BLE. This had ornamental sideplates and was profusely engraved.

The different guns can be categorised using the model names familiar to many owners and grouped into the sidelock range and the boxlock range. The tables on pages 93-94 are an attempt to clarify this rather confusing position and to indicate to owners the relative position of their gun in the model hierarchy.

## Sidelocks

The top of the sidelock range was the Extra Quality Victor SLE. This gun was a best quality ejector built on a conventional bar-action sidelock mechanism. The name Victor was introduced in 1879 as the Victor Hammerless and the first guns were back-action sidelocks built on Scott and Baker's 1878 patented hammerless action. William Scott and Thomas Baker's Patent No. 761 of 23 February 1878 describes a mechanism that uses hooks on the barrel flats to draw forward cocking rods running through the body of the action. These cock the hammers when the gun is opened.

The patent describes a number of ways in which the movement of the cocking rods could be used to cock the hammers. In one, the hammers are powered by helical springs that surround the cocking rods and as the rods are drawn forward a collar compresses the springs thus cocking the gun. William Middleditch Scott, son of William Scott, co-founder of Webley & Scott, was a Birmingham maker who built guns on this patent for London makers including Holland & Holland and the action was made under licence by Cogswell & Harrison.

The later, bar-action sidelock Victor was offered with a variety of options. The

16-bore single barrel
rotary underlever
hammergun No. 9898,
completed in February
1881.

Photo: David Grant

company's 1900 catalogue lists 12-, 16- and 20-bore versions fitted with single or
double triggers for the same price of 55 guineas cash. They had automatic safeties
and a choice of steel or damascus barrels fitted with a treble grip and extended rib.
The single trigger mechanism used was originally Edgar Harrison's 1895 design and
contemporary advertisements claim it as the Victor Single Trigger.

After 1890 there exist examples of a single trigger mechanism where the barrel
selection is made using the safety catch very much as in a modern over-and-under
gun. The safety is pushed forward to fire the right barrel first and pulled backward
from the central position to fire the left barrel first. Of Edgar Harrison's numerous
ejector mechanisms, the one most commonly used for the Victor sidelock was the
1890 design protected by Patent No. 20,234. The mechanism uses the rocking
motion of the sidelock spring to raise a lever set in the front of the action which
trips the ejectors mounted in the fore end. A special grade of the Victor, the highly
decorated Modele de Luxe, was available for an extra 10 guineas. The company
proudly stated:

> This design of Gun has been made to meet the want of those Sportsmen who not
> only desire a Gun of the latest approved type of best quality workmanship, but also
> require that the weapon shall be artistic in appearance, being chased *en relief*, high
> engraved, very specially handsome stock, the chequering made of scroll design, very
> high finish, &c., and, in short, a *chef d'oeuvre*.

From 1912 the Victor was sold for 65 guineas cash under 'Special Condition of
Sale, which includes a six years' maintenance'. Part of the agreement was that the
guns should be serviced annually by the company for a fixed fee.

The Victor Pigeon Gun was another variant and only available in 12-bore for live
pigeon shooting. In the company's 1924 catalogue it is pointed out that the barrels
were specially bored for: 'strong shooting at the longest ranges, and even distribu-
tion at all distances'.

Victor grade guns for pigeon shooting were also sold as Grand Prix Pigeon Guns
to reflect the names of many of the British and European competitions that flourished prior to the abolition of live bird shooting in the 1920s. Grand Prix Pigeon
Guns were also built on other actions including a side-plated boxlock with Avant
Tout ejectors and assisted opening mechanism.

The Victor was sold from the 1890s up to the 1970s. Indeed, to celebrate its

190    THE FIELD 23 July 1970

# A gun for each century

## A London firm introduces the Victor and the Regency to mark its two hundredth birthday

To celebrate their bicentenary this year Messrs Cogswell and Harrison Limited, gunmakers of Piccadilly, London, have added two new game guns to their existing range. They are the Victor bicentenary model sidelock hammerless ejector, and the Regency bicentenary model boxlock hammerless ejector. Both have top lever actions, 2¼in chambered barrels, and, traditionally, have a straight hand stock.

The Victor sidelock has hand detachable locks, the high finish of which is a pleasure to see. Equally the polish which has been given to the bores of the barrels is admirable, and better than that found in many modern guns, which is distinctly rough if viewed under a microscope making leading more likely, and cleaning after firing more difficult.

The gun I was shown had 28in barrels, and weighed 6¾lb, which may be considered heavy for a modern game gun to be used for driven game shooting in this country. However, I prefer some weight in a gun, and, given good balance as in this instance, I feel its advantages in permitting the use of HV and 'maximum' loads in moderate comfort when required on bye-days outweighs its disadvantages.

### Full choke barrels

The trigger pulls were good and crisp. The game engraving is well executed, and refreshingly different from the more stereotyped fine scroll. The hand chequering of the stock and fore-end is in keeping with the high quality of the workmanship throughout. The price is £1,050 and barrel length, borings and stock measurement are to customer's order, as in all guns of this quality.

The Regency best quality boxlock, which I was allowed to see and shoot with, is a topping gun. It has 26in barrels, and weighs 6¼lb. Although I like a heavier gun, its balance and handling qualities were so good that I shot happily with it and, despite the full choke barrels, most successfully.

Here again finish and workmanship are excellent, and the heavy scroll engraving a pleasing touch for those who appreciate it and find that it adds to the enjoyment of their shooting and ownership of a gun. Its price is £500, but it is one of the few guns that I have test-fired as well as examined of which I can say without qualification that I would like to own.

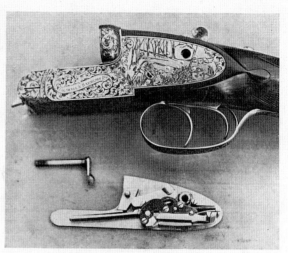

One of the bicentenary models: The Victor sidelock hammerless ejector has hand detachable locks, 28in barrels and weighs 6¾lbs. The price is £1,050 and barrel length, borings and stock measurements are to customer's order. Above, the lock plates and mechanism of the sidelock ejector. Below, the engraving on the barrel.

Victor bicentenary sidelock as featured in *The Field* of 21 July 1970.

bicentenary in 1970, Cogswell & Harrison reintroduced a special version of the famous Victor. The Victor Bicentenary Model [sic] was fitted with hand-detachable sidelocks and was custom built in respect of barrel length (25, 26 or 28 in.), boring and stock dimensions. Three chamber lengths were available in 12-bore. These were: 2¾, 2½ or 2 in. A variety of ribs were also available including Foulard (concave game rib), Churchill and raised file-cut.

The Victor Bicentenary Model was made to retail for £1,050 with a delivery of 12 to 18 months. Included in the price was free insurance for one year and free fitting at the West London Shooting Ground under the watchful eye of none other than Percy Stanbury. When reviewed in *The Field* on 23 July 1970, particular praise was made of the game scene engraving on the back of the locks and the bold scroll work on the bar, knuckle and fences 'refreshingly different from the more stereotyped fine scroll'. The accompanying illustration shows the words '1770 Victor Bicentenary Model 1970' inlaid in gold in the rib. By 1973 inflation had raised the price of a Victor to £2,000 and to £2,200 for one with hand detachable locks.

The 1900 catalogue also lists the Victor hammerless non-ejector quality gun. This catalogue appears to be the last existing record of a range of breech-loading hammer guns. They were supplied in a range of finishes from extra fine (45 guineas) to plain (20 guineas), the top of the range having either steel or damascus barrels and being fitted with rebounding locks. A 1912 catalogue lists the Crown sidelock ejector for 40 guineas in addition to the Victor.

The company's 1924 catalogue introduces the new Tower sidelock to the range

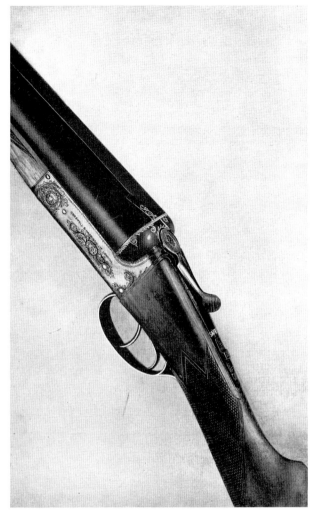

which at 70 guineas was priced between the established Victor (100 guineas) and the bottom of the range Crown (45 guineas). 1929 saw yet another addition to the range in the form of the Huntic, which occupied the bottom of the range below the Crown. In 1924 the range of sidelocks consisted of four guns commanding a series of prices that reflected both the quality of materials and the finish:

The Markor (left) and the Huntic (right), as advertised in the 1959 catalogue.

| The Victor | 100 guineas | The Tower  | 70 guineas |
| The Crown  | 50 guineas  | The Huntic | 34 guineas |

Following the Second World War the complete range of Cogswell & Harrison guns, boxlocks, sidelocks and rifles, was rationalised and only three sidelocks remained: the Victor Game Gun, still the company's flagship model; the Primic, a similar gun of plainer finish and the established Huntic. The Primic was phased out in 1958 and a price list from February 1965 lists only the Victor 'De Luxe' at £771 17s 6d, the Victor Game Gun at £712 10s and the Huntic at £534 7s 6d. In 1973 the sidelock range was reduced to only the Victor.

## Moorgrey Guns

Prior to the take-over of William Moore & Grey in 1908, Cogswell & Harrison made some fine quality London sidelock ejectors which Moore & Grey sold under its own name. In the early 1920s Cogswell & Harrison, now the owners of William Moore & Grey, marketed what it called the 'Moorgrey' gun. This very inexpensive sidelock was at the other end of the price spectrum from those guns produced for Moore & Grey at the turn of the century. Only a few hundred of these guns appear to have been produced, with their production at a peak between 1921 and 1922, primarily in the 49,000 series. In the six months between October 1921 and March 1922 some 90 Moorgrey guns were produced. The 1924 catalogue shows that the range was then cancelled.

Whilst the Moorgrey was an interesting experiment it seemed to fall between two stools. The guns were robust and functional but unattractive in appearance, some would say ugly, and lacked the simple elegance of the cheapest conventional boxlocks, even the simple non-ejector Markor. The idea of an uncomplicated sidelock did not fit in with the perceived wisdom of the boundaries between sidelocks and boxlocks.

The Moorgrey guns were also an attempt by Cogswell & Harrison to have a range of guns which could be sold off the shelf, with a limited range of specification options to provide an alternative to cheap foreign guns. Contemporary company documents state:

'The great aim in the design of the Moorgrey gun has been to produce a very strong wear resisting gun, at the same time to simplify the construction of an ordinary hammerless weapon in such a way that it can be produced at a very low price without sacrificing good workmanship and excellence of material. The great strength in the design of the breech action lies in it being about one third longer than usual whilst the lumps have one third greater bearing surface on the joint pin. The gun is fitted with side-locks, which are easily detachable by removing the sidepiece: each lock forms an independent unit, and can be taken off or put on without disturbing any other part of the mechanism.'

Since the guns were off the shelf, customers were limited to a series of options. Boring was limited to full choke, three-quarter or quarter choke in the left barrel and quarter choke or improved cylinder in the right. Likewise the English stocks were straight or half pistol grip hand and were of three lengths: short (14¼ in.), medium (14⁷/₁₆ in.) or long (14⁵/₈ in.) with the bend at the comb between 1³/₈ and 1⁵/₈ in.

The gun was offered in 12- or 16-bore. The weight of the 12-bore with 30 in. barrels was 6 lb 12 oz and the 16-bore with 27½ in. barrels was 6 lb 4 oz. The barrel length was limited to 30 or 27½ in. for the 12-bore and 27½ in. for the 16-bore. The simplest type T50 model, a non-ejector with automatic safety and snap forend was £13 10s. T51, the self-ejector, was £15 while the engraved T52 model with better finish and a figured stock was £20. There was also a Moorgrey wildfowl gun with 2¾ in. chambers proofed for 1¼ oz and with 30 in. barrels or supplied with specially choked 32 in. barrels. These were simple unsophisticated guns and their position in the hierarchy may be judged by the fact that the simplest conventional non ejector boxlock of the time cost 13 guineas, the Markor ejector model 15 guineas and the Rex 24 guineas.

Despite the commendable principles and an attempt at minimalism from which the idea was conceived, the Moorgrey was never really successful and although advertised in the 1924 catalogue, it was discontinued shortly thereafter.

The experiment in 'minimalism'.

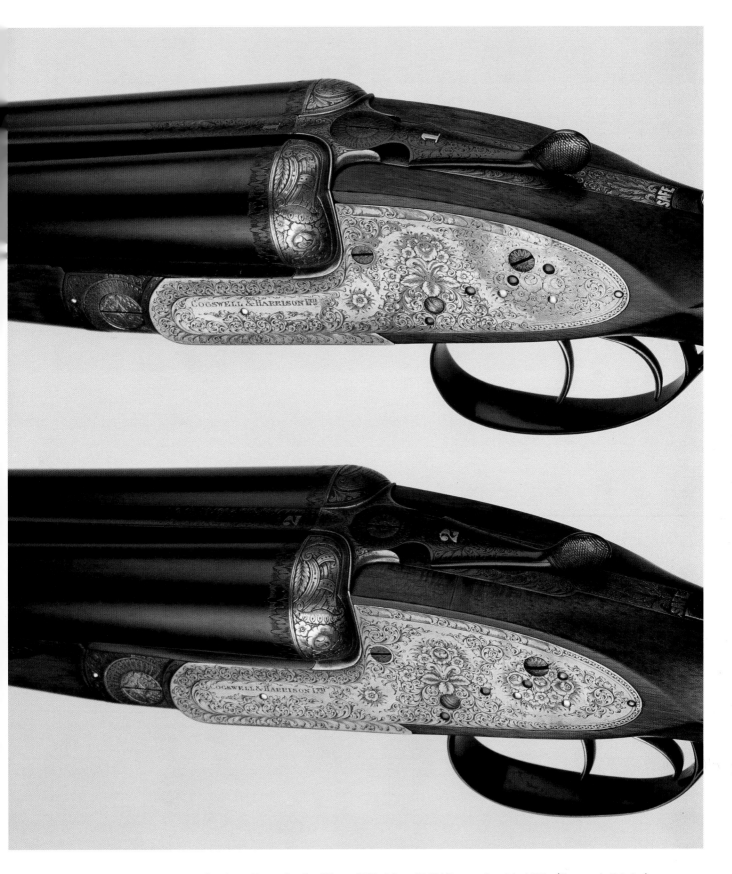

Plate 11 A matched pair of 12-bore Extra Quality Victor SLEs, Nos. 47,421/2, completed in 1920. *(Courtesy A. Brierley.)*

Plate 12

(above) A 12-bore boxlock fitted with Southgate ejectors, No. 55,181. It was sold from the Exeter shop on 18 December 1925. (*J. Newton collection.*)

(left) Cogswell & Harrison gun cases.

## Boxlocks

Cogswell & Harrison's first hammerless boxlock gun was the Desideratum for which advertisements exist from 1879 but in common with many early guns, no company illustration exists of this gun. It is known that it was built using a combination of the Gibbs and Pitt action and a Purdey type bolt.

The Gibbs and Pitt design uses extensions at the rear of the Purdey type bolt to force back the tumblers when the top-lever is turned to open the gun. The design was protected by Patent No. 284 of 1873 and during its life was licensed to a host of London and provincial gunmakers. Top lever cocked guns are often characterised by the length of the lever necessary to achieve the force necessary to move the tumblers into the cocked position. Cogswell & Harrison also used the top lever cocking mechanism to great effect in some sidelock guns.

The name 'Avant Tout' has become synonymous with Cogswell & Harrison and was first used for a range of self-ejecting hammer guns as early as 1888. Edgar Harrison's ejector design as used for the early sidelock actions was protected by Patent No. 16,214 of 10 December 1886 and was his first successful patent for an ejector mechanism. Although the mechanism was non-selectively tripped, it had a separate ejector mechanism for each barrel and with other contemporary designs marked the beginning of the development of the fully selective ejection mechanism with which we are familiar today.

The principle of the design was to use a rod, connected at one end to the tumbler,

Advertisement from *Dissertation on Guns and Shooting* (1906) for the Victor sidelock and the range of Avant Tout ejector guns.

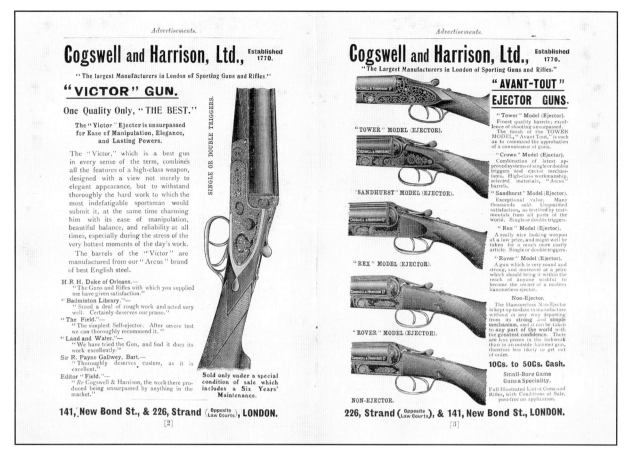

which passes through the body of the action and acts on an ejector trip protruding from the base of the front barrel lump. Interestingly, the early Avant Tout hammer guns were advertised by 'E. Harrison and Co. (Cogswell & Harrison), 226 Strand London W.C.' This was the subsidiary company owned by Edgar Harrison and Julia Chaplin which manufactured and sold guns from Cogswell & Harrison under its own name. John Peskett's history of the company, *Bicentenary of a Gunmaker*, records that E. Harrison & Company also made a less expensive range of guns including the Colonialist hammer or hammerless for 12 guineas, a Special at 10 guineas and a Keeper or Farmer's gun at 8 guineas.

The Avant Tout ejector hammer guns were soon followed by hammerless boxlocks and from 1896 the name Avant Tout began to be used to describe the company's range of boxlock guns. The company's 1900 catalogue advertising the 'Cogswell & Harrison's System of Ejector Guns' uses a simple illustration of the ejector mechanism described in Edgar Harrison's 1888 Patent No. 11,550, and from this basis, the Avant Tout hammerless ejector action became the cornerstone of the company's range of guns up until the early 1970s. However, the Avant Tout mechanism was also used on some of the less expensive sidelocks.

The initially bewildering confusion of names and advertising hyperbolae doesn't make it easy to understand which guns were and which were not of the Avant Tout type. Advertisements in Edgar Harrison's 1906 book *A Dissertation on Guns and Shooting* lists four Avant Tout hammerless ejector guns. The Crown retailed for 40 guineas, the Sandhurst fitted with ornamental sideplates was available with double

triggers for 26 guineas or a single trigger for 28
guineas. The Rex was also available with double or
single triggers for 20 and 22 guineas respectively and
the Ideal model at 15 guineas cash. Similarly advertisements in the 1908 version of the book *Guns and
Shooting* list five guns built on the Avant Tout hammerless action. This time the top of the range is the
Tower followed by the Sandhurst, the Rex and the
Rover. Also included is a boxlock non-ejector without a name.

The company's French catalogue of 1906 similarly
lists the Avant Tout Modele Sandhurst at 700 Fr, the
Modele Rex at 525 Fr and the Avant Tout at 400 Fr.
By the time the 1912 British catalogue came out, the
Crown was reappearing as a sidelock ejector and no
mention is made of the Avant Tout. Surviving copies
of the 1924 and 1929 catalogues make no reference
at all to the Avant Tout, either as a hammerless ejector action or as a specific model. The names previously prefixed by Avant Tout are simply referred to
as ejector guns; the same is true of the 1929 catalogue.

In 1949 the Avant Tout series reappears in the
form of the Konor (Avant Tout I), Sandhurst (Avant
Tout II) and Rex (Avant Tout III) ejector guns. All
are boxlocks, or 'enclosed locks' to quote the catalogue, although the Konor was fitted with ornamental sideplates which were claimed to strengthen the
head of the stock and give added surface area for
engraving. The catalogue recounts the history of the
name:

The Sandhurst from
the 1959 catalogue.

> The 'Avant Tout' hammerless ejector guns first came into production in 1896 –
> many thousands were sold – their popularity was unbounded – and even today, we
> are asked for this well known model. The 'Konor', 'Sandhurst' and 'Rex' were of
> this series and today are known by their individual names but have been greatly
> improved making them the finest guns in the world, made to withstand the hard
> work to which most indefatigable sportsmen would submit them, at the same time
> charming the users with their ease of manipulation, beautiful balance and reliability.'

The series was overhauled in the 1960s when the Konor and Rex were discontinued and replaced with the Blagdon (Avant Tout III) ejector, which was no longer
listed in the 1973 catalogue. The Konor survives the misfortune of the Blagdon
boxlock but has vanished by the 1978 catalogue.

In its original form, the Avant Tout action was the vehicle chosen by Edgar
Harrison to introduce a number of developments, including improvements to his
first ejector mechanism in the form of two patents: No. 18,157 of 1888 and No.
13,591 of 1889. The action was also available with one of the first single trigger
mechanisms fitted to effectively overcome the problem of double discharge, Edgar
Harrison's 1895 Patent No. 4,005.

12-bore Blagdon with the patented single trigger. No. 24,946, it was completed on 19 January 1901.

Courtesy of 'Kernow'

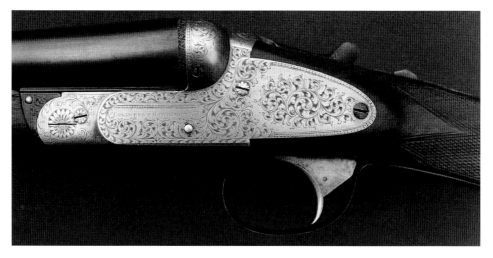

The Konor (left) and the Rex, from the 1959 catalogue.

There remain thousands of Avant Touts in use world-wide, giving sterling service, many over 100 years old and are testimony to the reliability of the design. The company recognises that if the Avant Tout had been designed and introduced today, it would be regarded as an important gunmaking innovation. That it was introduced at the end of the nineteenth century, demonstrates Edgar Harrison's ingenuity. For

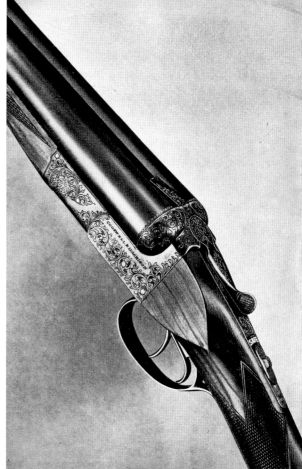

the first time his unique design put English boxlocks within the reach of those of modest means. It facilitated the introduction of a reliable ejector mechanism in guns available across a range of prices from simple workaday guns to high grade sideplated boxlocks.

During the latter half of the nineteenth century Cogswell & Harrison recognised that with the social and political changes in society, increasing numbers of the public had the opportunity to shoot but could probably not afford the cost of the top of the range guns such as the Victor. So in 1879 Edgar Harrison laid the foundations for the company's future manufacturing policy around the forerunner to the Avant Tout when he introduced the Desideratum. An advertisement from 1879 declared:

> Cogswell & Harrison, having laid down special machinery for the manufacture of these guns, are in a position to turn them out in a superior style. A judicious admixture of hand labour is used for fitting the parts and shaping up the iron and wood thus ensuring accurate fitting and symmetrical appearance throughout the whole.

*The Field* at that time declared the Desideratum to be a 'good and simple hammerless gun at a moderate price'. These moderate prices were a result of the 'close to form' manufacturing techniques employed by Cogswell & Harrison. Edgar Harrison was impressed by the techniques employed by American manufacturers who used machines to form the component parts to a uniform size. This left the skilled workman the hand finishing to fit the parts together and the results were a more consistent product at a reduced cost. Edgar Harrison was so impressed by the techniques employed by company's like Smith & Wesson he introduced similar

An advertisement for the Konor sideplated boxlock from the June 1961 issue of *Guns Review* magazine.

machinery and methods to his company's London factory. Some people questioned the quality when the technique was applied to best quality London guns but Edgar Harrison's opinion was that: '. . . it is the last cut of the file that requires the most judgement, and the last cut still remains'.

In his 1908 book *Experts on Guns and Shooting* the Editor of *Land and Water* magazine, G.T. Teasdale-Buckell, outlines Edgar Harrison's philosophy further:

> There are 400 different machining operations necessary to the making of a single gun. When they have been performed the skilled worker is called in. He collects the pieces and builds up the gun, but not before each part has been gauged in every possible way, and touched with the hand-tool as it may require.

Harrison, in his book *A Dissertation upon Guns and Shooting* published in 1906, anticipated the manufacturing techniques which only recently have been accepted by modern London gunmakers for the close-to-form production techniques now used to produce many of the components of best quality London guns. The modern approach takes advantage of advances in machine tool technology and makes use of such innovations as CNC (computer numerical controlled) equipment and spark erosion techniques. In his day, Harrison concluded:

> Special machinery has greatly facilitated the carrying out of this policy. In fact it has gone so far that in many of the best organised factories, the early processes of fashioning a gun are identically alike, irrespective of whether the gun will be ultimately finished as a best or medium grade production.

---

## 27½ in. Barrels

When thinking of standard or conventional barrel lengths for London guns, 30 in. and then 28 in. come to mind. Several options were of course available as London guns were bespoke. However, convention resulted in 28 or 30 in. barrels being recommended and were usually chosen by the customer. Other barrel lengths were associated with particular makers. Churchill's advocacy, some would say his defence, of 25 in. barrels will always associate this length and distinctive narrow rib with that maker. In the same vein but to a lesser extent, Woodward comes to mind when 29 in. barrels are mentioned.

If Cogswell & Harrison could be associated with a particular barrel length other than the conventional 28 and 30 in., it would undoubtedly be 27½ in. Indeed, this is a notable feature of the record books in the 1930s. The 27½ in. length barrels were supplied in all bore sizes and the number in twelve bore is striking. They were supplied across the model range but were particularly popular with those purchasing the Sandhurst model. They were usually fitted with a sunken rib and had a slightly reduced wall thickness made for 'lightweight barrels'. When struck up and fitted to the action

they would typically weigh around 2 lb 12 oz. By contrast 28 in. barrels would typically weigh around 3 lb and 30 in. barrels about 3 lb 2 oz.

The 27½ in. barrels were midway in length between the obviously short 25 in. and the standard 30 in. barrels. They certainly made for a light 12-bore. The 12-bore Sandhurst model weighed between 6 lb 2 oz and 6 lb 6 oz. The short barrels were made for a light and fast-handling gun that suited a more spontaneous form of shooting. With a 1 oz load they were easy on the shoulder and were a light and biddable companion in the field.

Being ½ in. shorter than 28 in. barrels probably did not make much practical difference. At the psychological level, their distinctiveness clearly appealed to a small but dedicated following. One of the finest natural self taught shots in the West of Ireland whose prowess at snipe and woodcock shooting was legendary in his community, would swear that it was all down to his 27½ in. Coggie.

Teasdale-Buckell is in no doubt regarding Harrison's enthusiasm for the manufacturing technology:

> Mr. Harrison has no love of the salesman's business. . . Some new piece of machinery or some new tool has more charm for him than the finished article. He holds that perfection of machinery insures perfect parts of a gun, and that it is only when all the individual parts are perfect that a perfect whole is possible. . . No gunmaker in London sees more, or perhaps, as much, of his guns as Mr. Harrison does. He sees that each machine is turning out its work correctly, and when that is done he is of the opinion that the finished article is within measurable distance, and can hardly go wrong.

By far the commonest type of repair currently undertaken by Cogswell & Harrison is the adjustment and regulation of boxlocks and assisted opening boxlock ejectors built on the Avant Tout action. The majority of these result from the guns being incorrectly regulated by gunsmiths unfamiliar with Edgar Harrison's simple and innovative designs, most noticeably the ejectors and the single trigger mechanism.

The Avant Tout design was straightforward, efficient and robust. It is clear that a number of common mistakes are possible when regulating the Avant Tout action. In particular, length is critical when fitting a new mainspring because on firing, the spring moves forward just sufficient for the inertia to engage the ejector sear. Once the mainspring is correctly fitted and regulated the mechanism is simple and reliable. If a mainspring of incorrect length is fitted, the spring can impede the working of the ejector mechanism. Should the owner then experience difficulties with ejection, blame might be laid unfairly on the mechanism's design. The true position is that a gunsmith may have unwittingly caused the problem. By understanding the mechanism properly, the Avant Tout can be regulated like clockwork.

The key to understanding the operating principles of the ejector mechanism described in Edgar Harrison's Patent No. 11,550 of 10 August 1888, is to appreciate the role played by the mainspring in the simple mechanism. When an Anson and Deeley type boxlock gun is fired, the main spring moves forward. It is quite straightforward to modify the forward end of the spring and use it to trip the ejector mechanism.

Referring to the illustration in the *Shooting with Game and Gun-room Notes*, we can see that two sears (A), one for each ejector, are hinged in the forend (C). The forward part of the sear can engage in a notch cut in the

Details of the Patent Ejector from *Shooting with Game and Gun-room Notes.*

ejector leg (D). On firing the gun the mainspring, shown compressed, moves forward within the body of the action against the sear, which since it is hinged, depresses the rear and raises the front into the notch cut in the ejector leg. On opening the gun, the mainspring is withdrawn from the rear of the sear during the action of cocking the tumbler.

When the gun is open enough for the cartridge head to clear the face of the action, a projection toward the rear of the sear is arrested by a recess cut in the knuckle in

The Avant Tout
mechanism as
described in the text.
Note the ejector box
on the underside of
the barrels.

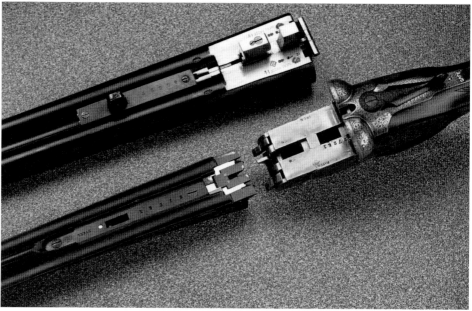

Photo: David Grant

front of the hinge pin, and depresses the front of the sear, withdrawing it from the notch in the ejector leg. The spring-powered ejector (E) is then released, throwing the spent cartridge clear.

On opening a gun which has not been fired, the mainspring will not have moved forward and engaged with the sear which remains in its normal position and away from the notch in the ejector leg. So when the gun is opened the ejector travels slowly, only raising the head of the cartridge from the chamber for extraction. A later patent, No. 18,157 of 12 December 1888, further developed the ejector theme with the addition of cocking the gun and ejecting the spent cartridge at the same time. Harrison's later patents, No. 13,591 of 1889, show three different ejector mechanisms all using the forward motion of the mainspring.

It is an interesting, if somewhat academic exercise, to speculate whether the British gun trade could have continued producing modestly priced boxlocks with the feel and balance of a high quality London-made gun if the manufacturing philosophy of men like Edgar Harrison had been further developed following the Second World War. The influx of quality machine-made foreign guns, which contributed to the

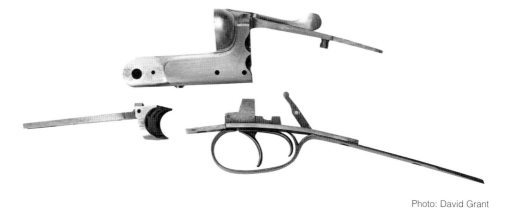

Components for an
Avant Tout scroll back
12-bore boxlock
ejector.

Photo: David Grant

demise of the British guntrade, may not have occurred on the same scale as it did if
there had been more robust home-grown competition.

In addition to the range of Avant Tout boxlocks, Cogswell & Harrison manufactured the Markor and the General Purpose hammerless boxlock ejectors. The
Markor name was first introduced in 1926 and appears in the surviving 1929 catalogues, where it is used for the company's cheapest hammerless boxlock at £13 10s
for the non-ejector and £15 15s for the ejector. The Markor survives into the 1965
price list where, although not illustrated in the accompanying catalogue, it is listed
at £159. The last catalogue entry for the Markor describes it as 'Rigid and Reliable'
and 'the ideal knock-about gun'.

The General Purpose gun intended for wildfowl and pigeon shooting first
appeared in Cogswell & Harrison's 1900 catalogue and survived as late as the 1949
price list. It was available only in 12-bore with 32 in. barrels and chambered for
either 2¾ or 3 in. cartridges. Originally intended as a work-a-day gun for the farm
or marsh, the General Purpose is listed in the 1929 catalogue in three grades of finish; Konor, Sandhurst and Rex. This precedes the use in 1949, of the same names
to describe the series of Avant Tout hammerless ejectors; Konor (Avant Tout I),
Sandhurst (Avant Tout II) and Rex (Avant Tout III).

Worthy of note was the Vena Contracta gun in which the barrel chambered for a
12-bore cartridge contracts down to 20-bore within the first third of its length. It was
designed by H. F. Phillips on 15 June 1893, Patent No. 11,828. Peskett reported that
Phillips was Cogswell & Harrison's Works
Manager at that time but there is some doubt
about this. The intention was to produce a
lighter, better handling gun but in practice the
idea failed to catch on although for a period of
time guns of this design were manufactured by
Langs.

An advertisement for
the Markor boxlock
from *Game & Gun*,
1926.

## The Certus Folding Gun

Photo: David Grant

Most sportsmen can remember vividly their first gun. For many who grew up on farms and in rural areas it was quite often a Certus single barrel .410 folding gun. They were very popular in the post Second World War period. This gun had a 28 in. barrel and was chambered to take 3 in. cartridges and also the ordinary 2½ or 2 in. .410 cartridges. It had a semi hammer (rebounding) mechanism and side lever with a nicely finished stock and handpiece. By depressing a small catch the weapon folded into a very convenient size 'for carrying in the car, pocket or suitcase'. One may suspect that the odd poacher or pothunter might also have found it very convenient to conceal.

The early models were attractive little guns and, as the company literature puts it, 'made entirely from British material by gunmakers who have had over 150 years experience of the small arms trade'. However, no pretence is made that the .410, even in its De Luxe form is an important example of gunmaking. It was simple, pleasurable and obtainable at a price within the reach of ordinary families.

The .410 still gives enormous pleasure to the thousands of sportsmen who retain one as a reminder of youthful forays in the field such as creeping up on rabbits in Spring, controlling vermin around the farm and potting pigeons. These early field craft experiences are an excellent preparation for an aspiring sportsman.

The Certus folding model was also available in 12-,16- and 20-bore. The 12-bore was chambered for 2¾in. cartridges and available with either 30 or 32 in.

barrel. The 20-bore was chambered for a standard 2½ in. cartridge and the barrel was 28 in. long.

In 1949 the .410 version cost £10 plus tax. For many years these guns were truly British made. However, at a later period they were based on imported guns and the quality and overall finish did not compare well with the earlier versions.

# 15 Over-and-Under Shotguns

Despite being one of the oldest London gunmakers and having such a record of innovation and technological achievement the company produced very few over-and-under shotguns.

In the 1934 publication *Special List of Best Guns* Cogswell & Harrison announced the availability of their 'Under and Over'. Two types were offered: a sidelock ejector at 110 guineas and a boxlock ejector at 60 guineas. By way of comparison, the Victor sidelock ejector game gun with hand detachable locks cost 100 guineas.

No illustration of the over-and-under gun was included in the document. However, the announcement was tantalising but, when a search of the 1934, 1935 and 1936 records was undertaken, no records were found of over-and-under guns in that period. It is reasonable to speculate that the announcement was to test the market.

A search of the company archive reveals that not until the 1937 records are two over-and-unders listed: a sidelock ejector No. 57,434 and a boxlock ejector No 57,435. It would appear that work had been done intermittently on these during the previous two or three years.

Although work on both guns commenced on 24 September 1937, it is believed that work was suspended for the duration of the Second World War. The sidelock was finally completed on 16 October 1945 and was described as being profusely engraved, fitted with an automatic safety, double triggers and the locking mechanism included a cross-bolt. The forend was in two pieces, reminiscent of some German guns, with the upper section fixed to the barrels and the lower part detachable by means of a push-button Deeley-type mechanism. The records show that the barrels for the sidelock were choked twenty-five thousands of an inch, or 'points' of choke, in the lower barrel and twenty-six in the upper barrel.

In the case of the boxlock, of which there are no contemporary or modern photographs, we do know the stock length, bends and cast offs. The weight of the 27½ in. barrels (both bored full choke) when fitted to the action is given as 3 lb 1 oz and the overall weight of the finished gun as 6 lb 11 oz.

It appears that the boxlock was stored during the war and was still with the company in 1945. The 1947 entry in the company archives records double triggers and a non-automatic top safety. The gun was sold on 18 June 1947 following some modifications and minor 'repairs'. The price was £175, which was a considerable sum in post-war Britain. It is reasonable to speculate that Cogswell & Harrison was considering an entry into this segment of the market and was experimenting with these two comparatively light guns. The boxlock weighed 6 lb 11 oz and its 27½ in. barrels 3 lb 1 oz.

During the early stage of research on this book, Mr John Congram located the sidelock model and allowed us to photograph it. It will be seen from the illustration that the action is more of a continental form as represented by the crossbolt locking. The forend had its top sections fixed to the barrels and the main section was removable by means of a push button Deeley type mechanism. The barrels were fitted with a raised solid rib.

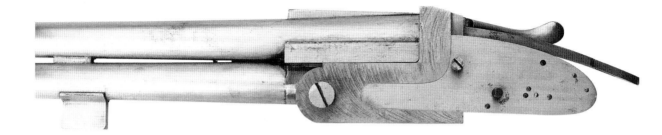

20-bore Woodward type over-and-under in the early stages of manufacture.

It would seem that Cogswell & Harrison produced only the two over-and-under shotguns although a craftsman who worked for the company believes he saw other actions being worked on.

The use of these continental-type actions reflects the way in which the company would sometimes cautiously try out a market by getting 'bought in' items before fully committing manufacturing resources. This was the case when the company was experimenting with autoloaders and also some magazine rifles where a few actions were bought from Steyr in Austria. This also seemed to have been done with the over-and-unders and presumably, as in the two cases cited above, the company decided not to set up its own facilities and enter the market.

## Sjörgen Autoloader

Edgar Harrison was always keen to keep abreast of the latest developments in gun design and manufacturing techniques. He did not preclude the consideration of guns that were well outside the London gunmaking tradition. A case in point is his interest in autoloading guns. As early as 1901, his fertile mind was working on such mechanisms and his innovations resulted in Patent No.13,382, Improvements Relating to Recoil Operated firearms.

The Sjörgen mechanism was based on a 1902 patent relating to a self-loading rifle. The shotgun version necessitated changes to Sjörgen's original design in order to accommodate a tube magazine and pivoted cartridge lifter for the feed mechanism. The record books show that several Sjörgen autoloaders bore the Cogswell & Harrison name on special barrels that were London proofed.

For reasons not evident from the records, the experiment with the Sjörgen autoloaders did not continue. Perhaps the gap between this form of shotgun and those of the traditional London Gun Trade was too wide to bridge. Furthermore, there was no significant demand for autoloading guns at the time. The trade had to await the post-war growth of clay pigeon shooting before there were any worthwhile markets in the UK.

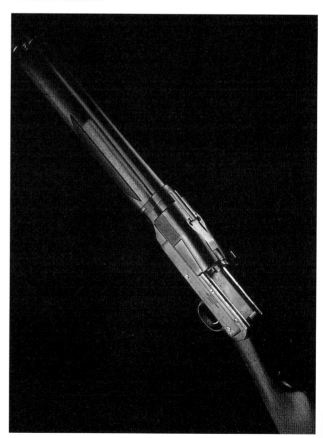

## Sidelock Range of Hammerless Guns

| Model | Year In Catalogue (i) | Ejector | | Trigger | | Bore (ii) |
|---|---|---|---|---|---|---|
| | | Ejector | Non-ejector | Double | Single | |
| Victor | 1900–1978 | Yes | | Yes | Yes | 12, 14, 14³/₄, 16, 20 |
| Modele de Luxe & | 1900–1973 | Yes | | | | 12, 14, 16, 20 |
| Victor Pigeon Gun | 1900–1924 | Yes | | Yes | Yes | 12 only |
| Victor Non-ejector | 1900 | | Yes | Yes | | 12, 16 & 20 |
| Victor Small Bore | 1900–1978 | Yes | | Yes | Yes | 28 |
| Primic - plain finish Victor | 1949 | Yes | | Yes | Yes | 12, 16 & 20 |
| Crown | 1912–1929 | Yes | | Yes | Yes | 12, 14³/₄, 16 & 20 |
| Tower | 1924–1929 | Yes | | Yes | Yes | 14³/₄, 16 & 20 |
| Huntic | 1929–1965 | Yes | | Yes | Yes | 12 &16 |
| Moorgrey[1] | 1919–1924 | Yes | Yes | Yes | | 12 & 16 |

1 Moorgrey model discontinued prior to 1924 catalogue.

**Notes:**

The tables on pages 93 and 94 relate to catalogue contents only and are for the guidance of researchers and collectors. They are not, therefore, a complete list of guns that were built by Cogswell & Harrison.

(i) The year of the catalogue does not coincide with the year the gun was first produced. For example, the Victor hammerless was introduced in 1879 but appeared in the 1900 catalogue, which was the earliest one available in the archive.

(ii) Several of the sidelocks were built as 28-bore and 410s.

**Boxlock Range of Shotguns**

| Model | Year In Catalogue | Action | | Ejector | | Trigger | | Bore |
|---|---|---|---|---|---|---|---|---|
| | | Boxlock | Side-plated | Ejector | Non-ejector | Double | Single | |
| Desideratum | 1879 | Yes | | | Yes | Yes | | 12, 16 & 20 |
| General Purpose[1] | 1900–1949 | Yes | | Yes | Yes | Yes | | 12 |
| Blagdon – single trigger | 1900 | Yes | Yes | Yes | | Option | Yes | 12, 16 & 20 |
| Avant-Tout Inc. | | | | Yes | Yes | Yes | Yes | 12, 16, 20 & 28 |
|     Light Model | 1900 | Yes | | Yes | | Yes | Yes | 28 |
|     Rover | 1912 | Yes | | Yes | Yes | Yes | | 12, 16 & 20 |
| Avant-Tout Series (Longfort[2] Breech action) | | | | | | | | |
|     I Konor | 1961–1973 | | Yes | Yes | | Yes | Yes | 12, 16 & 20 |
|     II Sandhurst | 1906–1965 | | Yes | Yes | | Yes | Yes | 12, 14¾, 16 & 20 |
|     III Rex | 1929–1965 | Yes | | Yes | | Yes | | 12, 16 & 20 |
|     III Blagdon | 1965 | Yes | Yes | Yes | | Yes | | 12, 16 & 20 |
| Markor | 1926–1965 | Yes | | Yes | Yes | Yes | | 12, 16 & 20 |
| Regency | 1970–1978 | Yes | | Yes | | Yes | | 12, 16 & 20 |
| Ambassador | 1978 | Yes | Yes | Yes | | Yes | | 12, 16 & 20 |
| Certus Single Barrel | 1949–1965 | Yes - exposed hammer | | | Yes | | Yes | 12 |
| Model 1 & 2 de Luxe | 1924–1965 | Yes | | | Yes | | Yes | .410 gauge |
| Model 4 | | | | | | | | |

1. General Purpose was a 3 in. chambered 12-bore for wildfowl and game at long ranges [sic], listed as available in 'Sandhurst' and 'Rex' qualities in the 1924 catalogue. The 1947 catalogue includes 2¾ in. chambered guns built for heavy charges, i.e. magnum. Regulated to shoot tight patterns.
2. Longfort (Regd.) breech action mentioned in 1946 catalogue for both shotguns and double rifles, reported that the increased distance between forward and rear lump provided improved lock-up and extra gape when open.

**Note:** 1924 and 1929 Catalogues do not refer to Avant Tout either as action type or as any specific gun.

# 16  Rifles

When the company was acquired in May 1993 it soon became clear that it would be an enormous research task to establish which products the company made and when. Associates and owners of Cogswell & Harrison guns were invited to send in details of interesting or unusual guns they owned or knew of. This revealed early on that the company had made a wide variety of shotguns both in terms of type, quality and cost. Around this time an American associate sent an advertisement from the summer 1993 issue of *Double Gun Journal*. The advertisement from Lewis Drake and Associates of Murray Kentucky was offering for sale a Cogswell & Harrison single barrel 4-bore rifle, serial No. 9176, for $27,500. The rifle was described in great detail and was a timely reminder that throughout its long history Cogswell & Harrison also made a wide variety of rifles: double rifles built on both sidelock and boxlock ejector and non-ejector actions, falling block rifles, bolt action magazine rifles, rook and rabbit rifles, a range of simple bolt action rifles for use around the farm and for target shooting and ball and shotguns.

To fully appreciate Cogswell & Harrison's range of rifles it is worth considering the historical development of the sporting rifle. The beginning of the nineteenth century saw the railways create new opportunities for travel both home and abroad. Sportsmen were quick to take advantage. The Victorians became interested in Scotland and the sport that could be had in the Highlands and the expanding Empire was taking soldiers and officials to new lands having a wide variety of game species, often dangerous. Gunmakers' expanded their range of weapons to meet the growing demand for the variety of rifle and rifle/shotgun combinations required by the sportsmen at home and abroad.

Prior to the beginning of the nineteenth century the rifle was almost universally a single barrel, muzzle-loaded flintlock weapon with either a smooth bored or rifled barrel, firing a patched ball. For hunting, the principal requirements of the rifle bullet/ball combination are velocity, penetration and killing power. To increase killing power, the normal practice was to increase the powder charge to raise the velocity. This led to 'stripping', where the lead ball was forced through the barrel at such a velocity that it would not take the spin of the rifling. As a consequence velocity had to be kept to a moderate level to ensure accuracy and the only way to increase the power was to use larger calibres, often smooth bored guns or guns with the rifling bored out.

This led to the widespread adoption of big bore rifles for hunting. 10-bore was considered a conservative choice whilst 8- or 4-bore was the normal choice for dangerous game. The invention in 1807 of the percussion ignition system by the Reverend Alexander Forsyth marked a major turning point for both the rifle and the shotgun. However, the almost instantaneous ignition and rapid burn of the main powder charge tended to increase velocities leading to an increase in stripping.

The quest to overcome this problem eventually led to significant developments in the art and science of both barrel boring and rifling. The most promising solution was the 'two-groove' rifling system in which the projectile had two projections or fins, which fitted into the two recessed grooves in the internal bore of the barrel.

This system allowed the projectile to be driven at higher velocities without the danger of stripping. Progressive rifling where the rate of twist increased progressively along the length of the barrel, achieved a degree of success in target rifles but proved to be less successful in sporting rifles.

The second half of the nineteenth century saw gunmakers experimenting with new materials and ideas, producing an amazing variety of weapons in a bewildering range of calibres. The introduction of nitro-cellulose based powders and the development of the capping breech loader were two significant milestones.

Probably the most important milestone for both the shotgun and the rifle came in 1851 when the Lefauchaux pinfire shotgun was exhibited at the Paris Exhibition. From this design evolved the improved pinfire and then the centrefire breech-loading shotguns. Rifle makers where at first reluctant to accept the new technology. The Lefauchaux design was barely able to withstand the pressures developed by shotgun cartridges let alone the high pressures of a rifle round. But despite the early reservations, technological developments and improvements in the design led to the acceptance of breech loading double rifles.

The replacement of damascus barrels made from alternating strips of steel and iron with those made entirely of steel similarly led to improvements. Steel could be cut into cleaner rifling and was more resistant to wear and corrosion particularly from the new nitro powders which were more corrosive than black powder.

The development of the bolt action rifle was closely linked to the principal military requirements of sustained firepower and mechanical reliability. As a design, the bolt action familiar to many of today's sportsmen emerged from the search by the nineteenth century's military powers for a reliable breech-loading rifle. Two military rifle actions emerged from the period to dominate the design of the bolt action sporting rifle. Both designs are bolt action repeating mechanisms, both are fed from a clip-type magazine and both continue to dominate today's sporting rifle market: the German Mauser and the Austrian Mannlicher.

The Mauser action was the product of the partnership between two brothers, Paul and Wilhelm Mauser. Paul worked in the Government firearms factory at Oberndorf in the Kingdom of Würtenburg and in 1867 developed his design for a bolt-action single shot rifle. The key to his design was four fold: the lock was self cocking; on opening the striker is retracted behind the bolt face preventing the possibility of premature ignition when loading a fresh cartridge; the bolt has both an extractor and ejector and a safety catch mounted on the cocking piece locks the bolt preventing the striker from reaching the cartridge.

The Austrian Mannlicher design differed from the Mauser in that the bolt was operated by a straight backwards and forwards movement but like the Mauser the action was cocked by lifting the bolt handle. Coupled with the straight-pull action was a box magazine that could be loaded using a clip holding five cartridges. One disadvantage of the straight-pull action was that telescopic sights had to be mounted using a side mount to avoid obstructing the bolt.

By the beginning of the twentieth century the sporting rifle had evolved into a highly accurate weapon available in a variety of styles and a range of calibres unimaginable to the early Victorian sportsman. Cogswell & Harrison were able to offer a range of weapons in a bewildering variety of calibres and finishes whether the sport was shooting vermin and rabbits around the farm, red deer in Scotland, sambar in the Indian hills or rhinoceros and elephant on the African savannah.

A Cogswell & Harrison sidelock ejector over-and-under, No. 57,434. Work commenced on 24 September 1937 but was suspended for the duration of World War Two. The gun was not completed and sold until 18 June 1947.
*(Courtesy J. Congram.)*

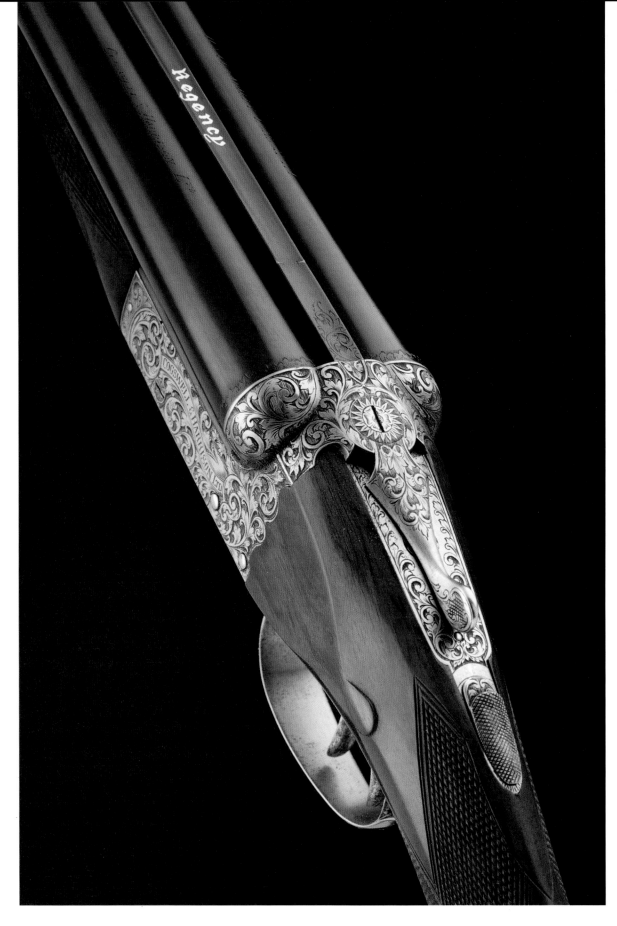

Plate 14 A 12-bore Regency, one of the 'Guns of Distinction' introduced in 1970 to commemorate the company bicentenary. This model is still available in all calibres.

## Double Rifles

In the 1830s and 1840s the double rifle was considered *the* game rifle by sportsmen who travelled the Empire in search of quarry. A single-barrelled rifle, although accurate at moderate ranges, took time to reload. This was a great handicap should a wounded deer escape and was likely to be fatal for the sportsman confronted with a wounded lion or rhinoceros. To meet the sportsman's requirements for a quick second shot the gunmakers came up with double rifles. For those who expected to face dangerous game at close quarters the large calibre double rifle became the weapon of choice. It was the double rifle's ability to fire two, often heavy calibre, bullets one after the other as fast as it was to aim and pull the triggers that made them popular. It was the difference between BANG-BANG and BANG-1-2-BANG.

The double rifle is still regarded by many as the epitome of the gunmaker's art. The high pressures generated require an action capable of withstanding the stresses developed at the interconnection of the action flats and the standing breech. The jointing of the barrels to the action must be first class and the locking mechanism robust enough to withstand the pressures generated when a tight-fitting bullet is forced down a rifled barrel at velocities in excess of 2,000 feet per second. A consummate level of skill is required to align and regulate the two barrels to shoot to a single point of aim from one set of sights. If the barrels are parallel, the right barrel will shoot to the right and the left barrel to the left. This is corrected by making the barrels converge toward the muzzles, the degree of convergence depending on the range at which the barrels are to be zeroed, typically 100 yards. In practice this is achieved by the barrels being rigidly jointed at the breech end, whilst at the muzzles they are soft jointed using solder.

A test group is shot and assessed to see if the barrels need to be wedged apart or squeezed together. This is accomplished by heating the barrels at the muzzle end to soften the solder. The process is repeated with minor alterations to the alignment of the barrels until an acceptable group is achieved following which the barrels are rigidly jointed and finished with a flat rib to take the sights. These are typically leaf sights for the various ranges and a fine bead or simple blade foresight. The company's 1912 catalogue goes to some lengths to explain to customers that

> Cogswell & Harrison are not only rifle manufacturers but rifle-barrel makers as well and, therefore in a position to offer our Customers weapons giving the highest possible accuracy of shooting.

Since the turn of the century Cogswell & Harrison had been offering an impressive range of high velocity double rifles. The company emphasised that the development of weapons was closely linked to developments in the ammunition.

> As rifle manufacturers, and in particular as rifle barrel makers, we have devoted quite an exceptional amount of time, skill and money so as to obtain the maximum results from the new kinds of smokeless, super high velocity cartridges.

Cogswell & Harrison's most popular calibres for double rifles were the .375 recommended as suitable for both hill shooting in India and deer stalking in Scotland and the medium to heavy calibres .400 and .475 for large game.

The company continued developing its range of double rifles and in the 1920s introduced new calibres including .470, .275 and .250. The rifles were built on a

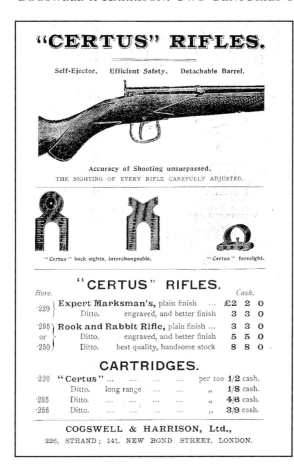

**"CERTUS" RIFLES.**

Self-Ejector.    Efficient Safety.    Detachable Barrel.

Accuracy of Shooting unsurpassed.
THE SIGHTING OF EVERY RIFLE CAREFULLY ADJUSTED.

"Certus" back sights, interchangeable.          "Certus" foresight.

**"CERTUS" RIFLES.**

| Bore. | | | Cash. |
|---|---|---|---|
| ·220 | **Expert Marksman's,** plain finish ... | £2 | 2 | 0 |
|  | Ditto.          engraved, and better finish | 3 | 3 | 0 |
| ·295 | **Rook and Rabbit Rifle,** plain finish ... | 3 | 3 | 0 |
| or | Ditto.          engraved, and better finish | 5 | 5 | 0 |
| ·250 | Ditto.          best quality, handsome stock | 8 | 8 | 0 |

**CARTRIDGES.**

| ·220 | "Certus" ... | ... | ... | ... | per 100 | 1/2 cash. |
|---|---|---|---|---|---|---|
|  | Ditto.  long range | ... | ... | " | 1/8 cash. |
| ·295 | Ditto. | ... | ... | ... | " | 4/8 cash. |
| ·256 | Ditto. | ... | ... | ... | " | 3/9 cash. |

**COGSWELL & HARRISON, Ltd.,**
226, STRAND; 141, NEW BOND STREET, LONDON.

Advertisement for the Certus Rifle.

range of actions and with a variety of finishes. The hammerless sidelock ejectors with detachable locks, elongated action strap and stalker's safety were top of the range. Boxlock ejectors were also available. Hammerless locks for double rifles were widely introduced from the 1880s. One advantage cited at the time was that hammerless guns were safer, especially when being carried by a native bearer. On the other hand external hammerlocks had several advantages: their simplicity of construction allowed them to be maintained and repaired in the bush; they could be cocked silently when stalking game. Also the second barrel could be left un-cocked to avoid the danger of a double discharge.

Interestingly the company did not use names (unlike its custom with shotguns) to differentiate between the various models of double rifle, although there were two exceptions. 'Longfort' was used to describe a particular action and later the action for the .375 Magnum model double rifle in the 1940s. 'Certus' was first used to describe Edgar Harrison's design for a bolt action magazine rifle and later for a variety of rabbit and rook rifles. In the 1960s, Longfort was used for a Mauser pattern bolt action rifle chambered for .30-06 and .308.

## Single Barrel and Magazine Rifles

The 'Certus' rifle manufactured by Cogswell & Harrison was Edgar Harrison's design for a bolt action magazine rifle protected by Patent No. 4,097 of 1 March 1900 entitled 'Improvements in Rifles'. The design was a hybrid between the conventional bolt action of the Mauser type and the straight pull of the Mannlicher-Schoenauer action. In its catalogue, the company quotes the Editor of *Land and Water* stating in its advertisement on 7 April 1900: 'The rifle action is not one that can be likened to that of any existing weapon, military or otherwise upon the market. While possessed of a bolt it is not the ordinary turn-bolt action,' before concluding, 'The diagram (of shooting) is first-rate.'

The same 1900 advertisement tells us that the 'Certus' was designed for the ' . . . sportsman requiring the advantages of a magazine rifle, combined with the high velocity smokeless powder cartridges, and heavy bullets.'

The advantages of the magazine rifle are accuracy and the multiple shot capability afforded by the magazine, whilst the .400 calibre 400 grain bullet for which the Certus was designed, could achieve a velocity exceeding that of a .303 but with a flatter trajectory. It would however, still deliver more stopping power than a .577 calibre bullet driven by 6 drams (164 grains) of powder, all with reduced recoil according to the company's literature. It is worth considering that a .577 black powder express cartridge driving a 570-grain bullet produced around 3,700-ft/lb energy. Many 'Certus' rifles were sold for use abroad and it is interesting to note the claims made for its use in India in the 1900 catalogue:

> The recent orders made in India under the Arms Act practically bar sportsmen from using rifles of service calibres and consequently it is an extra advantage that such a rifle as this will not subject its owner to many of the petty worries incidental to the possession of a weapon firing Service types of ammunition.

A 'Certus' sporting pattern rifle was also available in .22 and a bolt action rook and rabbit rifle in either .295 or .250 and all were available with interchangeable rear sights.

Cogswell & Harrison's French catalogue of 1907 lists a falling block rifle which although called the 'Certus', clearly had nothing to do with the design of the same name described above. The single shot falling block mechanism was operated by the downward movement of an underlever placed forward of the trigger guard. The breech-block slid downward exposing the chamber and when closed the breech-block was locked in place and the very nature of the design contributed to the accuracy. The most popular and celebrated falling block mechanism was the Farquharson patented in 1872 later to become inextricably linked with the name of the celebrated Bristol gunmaker George Gibbs.

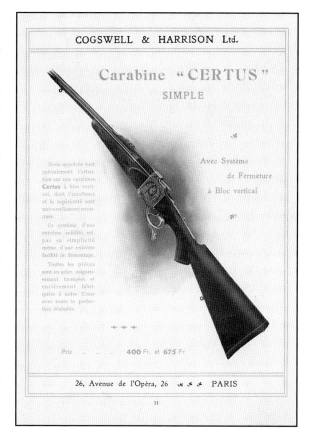

Advertisement from the Cogswell & Harrison French Catalogue of 1909 illustrating the Certus falling block rifle.

Bolt action weapons possess a very positive lock-up of the cartridge in the breech where the headspace is kept to a minimum. This ensures outstanding accuracy across the range of calibres. The different methods of locking the bolt in the closed position have produced an action which will safely withstand very high chamber pressures and as a direct consequence, bolt action rifles can be built in heavy calibres without the risk of a failure in normal use.

As the twentieth century progressed the company's catalogues listed more bolt action magazine rifles. The 1924 lists five: the .375 'Super High Velocity Rifle' with accompanying illustration showing a

Advertisement for the Certus rifle. The design for the Certus was protected by Edgar Harrison's 1900 Patent No. 4,097.

1956 advertisement for a bolt-action magazine rifle.

### COGSWELL & HARRISON LTD

# The 'Take Down' Model Rifle
#### MODEL B

This rifle has been designed to meet a demand for a weapon that can be easily transported and the barrel removed from the stock with the minimum of trouble, in fact, the removal of one screw only which can be loosened with an ordinary coin (see illustration below).

#### SPECIAL FEATURES

**BARREL.** 26 inch, Vickers "A" Steel, English nitro proof.

**ACTION.** Mauser type, fitted with light alloy magazine. Capacity four rounds, except calibre .404, which holds three rounds. Hinged floor plate with catch in trigger guard.

**FORESIGHT.** White metal tipped caterpillar pattern on long file cut ramp foresight block, fitted with tubular sight protector.

**REARSIGHT.** Three folding leaves, 100 yards, 200 yards, 300 yards. dovetailed into long file cut rib.

**APERTURE SIGHT.** Fitted to cocking piece with micrometer vertical and lateral adjustment, folding out of the way when open sights are used.

**STOCK.** Specially selected, well figured French walnut, full pistol grip, cheek piece, and fitted with "Silvers" rubber recoil pad.

**WEIGHT.** Approximately 8 lb., according to calibre.

**CALIBRES.** 7 mm., .275 Magnum, 30/'06 Springfield, .300 Magnum, .318 nitro express, 9.5 mm., .375 Magnum, .404, and 9.3 mm. Mauser.

BY TURNING ONE SCREW ONLY, BARREL AND ACTION CAN BE REMOVED

£95

28

### COGSWELL & HARRISON LTD

#### MODEL DE LUXE RIFLE
**Beautifully finished. Best quality material throughout.**

We have great pride in presenting this weapon for the discerning sportsman who insists on the best in everything.
It is impossible to do full justice to all the special features incorporated in its design, particularly as we are only too anxious to include the purchaser's special requirements. In general the outstanding points are as follows:—

**BARREL.** Length 26 in. or according to special requirements, made of Vickers steel and rifled with extreme precision to give long life with absolute accuracy.

**ACTION.** Mauser pattern, with low bolt handle to facilitate telescopic sight mounting. Fast cocking when bolt opened and fitted with positive safety on cocking piece. Heavily engraved as illustration.

**MAGAZINE.** Steel magazine with hinged floor plate and a capacity of three, four or five cartridges according to the calibre. Heavily engraved with scroll and bas-relief.

**STOCK.** Specially selected, highly figured French walnut of conventional or "Monte Carlo" pattern, fitted with a beaded cheek piece and full pistol grip, in which is incorporated a spare foresight in the highly engraved butt trap. Black horn tip to fore-end and a "Silvers" recoil pad to ensure maximum comfort when used under tropical conditions.

**FORESIGHT.** Caterpillar pattern with white metal bead ⅟₁₆ inch diameter fitted to a long ramp. file cut block, to eliminate light reflection, and a strong sight cover to guard against damage.

**REARSIGHTS.** All rifles have two patterns, the three-folding leaf iron sights being mounted in a long file cut top rib securely fixed to the barrel, sighted 100, 200 and 300 yards with a wide V and white line to facilitate sighting under adverse conditions.
The aperture sight is mounted on the cocking piece and is fitted with vertical and horizontal adjustment for elevation and windage.

**CALIBRES.** 7 mm., .275 Magnum, 30/'06 Springfield, .300 Magnum, .318 Express, 9.3 mm. Mauser, 9.5 mm. Nitro Express, .375 Magnum and .404 Nitro Express.
Other calibres made to order subject to special quotation.

£125.

29

Take Down Model Rifle (left) and Model De Luxe Rifle, from the 1959 catalogue.

conventional bolt action rifle which came fitted with a detachable barrel and was referred to as 'take-down' and described as 'The best all-round weapon of today'; there was a .275 'Super High Velocity Rifle' for soft skin medium to light game, recommended for Indian hill game and Scottish deer stalking and also came fitted with a detachable barrel as standard. Also listed was the .250/300 Savage, the .318 High Velocity and the .300 US cartridge magazine rifle.

Following the Second World War we again see in the 1949 Catalogue the .275 Super and the .375 Magnum for belted rimless cartridges. This is the first reference to the .375 in magnum load. Ammunition advertised in the same catalogue includes .470 Nitro-Express for double rifles, .375 and .275 in both belted rimless and flanged magnum configurations for double and magazine rifles respectively, .318 Super Velocity rimless for magazine rifles and 9.5mm High Velocity rimless.

The 1965 price list heralds the first widespread use of names to describe the range of magazine rifles: the 'Model de Luxe' model built on a conventional Mauser action, 'The Special', 'The Game Ranger', 'The Longfort', and 'The Sandhurst' which shared its name with a shotgun. There was also a degree of standardisation in the range of calibres available: 7 mm, .275 Magnum, .30-06 Springfield, .300 Magnum, .318 Express, 9·3 mm Mauser, 9·5 mm Nitro Express, .375 Magnum, .404 Nitro Express and .458 Winchester Magnum. The 1973 catalogue lists no Cogswell & Harrison rifles, the only British rifles on offer being from BSA and Parker Hale.

## 'Cosmos' Ball and Shotgun

To the uneducated eye Cogswell & Harrison's 'Cosmos' ball and shotgun looks and handles like a slightly heavy side-by-side shotgun fitted with rifle-type leaf sights marked for 50, 100 and 150 yards. A closer inspection would reveal coarse rifling for a length of approximately two inches at the muzzle of each barrel. Clearly no ordinary shotgun, the Cosmos was designed and built to be able to fire both shot and a solid projectile through the same barrels. It was advertised as the ideal all-in-one gun for the sporting gentleman at the turn of the century. The company's catalogue of 1900 proudly states that:

> The 'Cosmos' will be found a most excellent weapon to take abroad, as ball and shot may be fired from it with excellent results...takes the ordinary cartridge case for shot guns, and may be loaded with shot or ball - solid or express.

The Cosmos was offered in 8, 10, 12, 16 and 20 bore. The catalogue included a reproduction of the group fired before the Editor of *The Field*, which shows the impressive accuracy of guns of this kind. Ten shots from a 10-bore gun at 50 yards, using an 850 grain bullet driven by 8 drams of powder producing a muzzle velocity of 1,556 feet per second and yielding an energy of 4,564 ft lb, produced a group centred on an area of $2^{1}/_{2}$ by $3^{1}/_{8}$ in. So popular were these guns that, according to Peskett, the Maharaja of Jahore placed an annual standing order for two Cosmos guns. These were for the Maharaja to give as presents to favoured guests who had joined him on hunting trips.

The ball and shot gun was principally produced to meet the requirements of the colonial sportsman and those who travelled throughout the vast and diverse British Empire. The major difference between shooting at home and shooting in the colonies was the presence of large and often dangerous animals in addition to small game.

The Cogswell & Harrison archives show that gun No. 42,975 (Plate 9), was built as a 12-bore Cosmos ball and shot gun on an Avant Tout type boxlock ejector action with assisted opening mechanism and was completed on 23 September 1908. It has a conventional top lever, double triggers and an automatic top safety, light engraving throughout and a snap type forend. The barrels are $27^{1}/_{2}$ in. long and made of fine 'Arcus' steel. There are three leaf sights to 50, 100 and 150 yards. The barrels were nitroproofed at $1^{1}/_{8}$ oz and when struck up and fitted to the action weighed 3 lb 7 oz. The stock was originally $14^{9}/_{16}$" long with the bend at the comb $1^{1}/_{2}$ in. and at the heel 2 in. The stock cast offs were respectively zero, $^{1}/_{16}$ and $^{1}/_{8}$ in. When finished and assembled the gun weighed 7 lb 1 oz. The original purchaser took delivery of the gun on 19 March 1909 and paid 26 guineas for the privilege. In 1911, the gun was offered for re-sale through Cogswell & Harrison's London shop where it was sold on 23 October 1911 for 22 guineas.

It was for the same type of mixed shooting that the combination-guns referred to by the British gun trade as Cape guns or Cape rifles were made. Cape guns were double guns where one barrel was rifled and the other barrel was smooth-bored for shot. The Drilling is a similar combination gun, which remains popular with the European sportsman to this day. Guns with interchangeable barrels were also available to the travelling sportsman. The gun could be fitted with either a rifled or smooth-bored barrel depending on the anticipated quarry and manufacturers were able to offer a bewildering combination of calibres.

The simplest solution to the problem of mixed shooting was to be able to fire a solid projectile from a smooth-bored shotgun. In practice, however, a spherical ball fired from a smooth-bored barrel was inaccurate and limited in application to shooting at close range in thick jungle or from the back of an elephant. If the ball closely fitted the bore there were inevitably problems as the ball entered the choked region of the barrel. If on the other hand the ball was of a diameter small enough to pass through the restriction of the choke it would be loose fitting in the bore and the expanding gases driving it down the barrel would escape past it before it entered the choke. Initially, shotguns were either fitted with barrels bored cylinder along the entire length or an undersize ball was used with a patch of soft leather, which provided a gas check but was of sufficient compressibility to allow it to pass through the choke.

The solution to the problem came in the form of Patent No. 7,568 'Improvements in Gun-barrels' of 1885 taken out by the patent agent Henry Lake for George Vincent Fosbery, VC. After leaving Eton, George Fosbery obtained a commission in the Bengal Army of the Honourable East India Company in 1851 and during his service on the Northwest Frontier in 1863 won the Victoria Cross. Lieutenant Colonel Fosbery was an innovative man. Troops under his command on the North West Frontier fired explosive bullets of his design from their service Enfield rifles and he was responsible for a number of patents improving military weapons. His name is perhaps best remembered for the Webley-Fosbery automatic revolver developed by the Webley and Scott Revolver and Arms Co. Ltd from Fosbery's British patent No. 15,453 of 1895. The Webley-Fosbery design not only won honours in competition but saw extensive service as an officer's side arm.

The heart of Fosbery's 1885 patent was that the rifling necessary to stabilise the bullet in flight should be located within the short constriction of the choke where it would be sufficient to give the bullet spin, but not too excessive to disrupt the shot pattern. This was combined with bullets that would slide easily down the bore, offering minimal resistance until approaching the muzzle where a gentle forcing cone aligned them with the rifling which just gripped the bullets surface.

Fosbery's specification states that for a 12-bore gun the difference in calibre between the unrestricted barrel and the choked portion should be one millimetre or one twenty-fifth of an inch, and that the choked part of the barrel should be about one inch long. He specifies seven grooves in the choke with the grooves narrower than the lands between them and preferably four to six thousands of an inch in depth. In section the grooves are either semi-circular, square but ideally rounded and

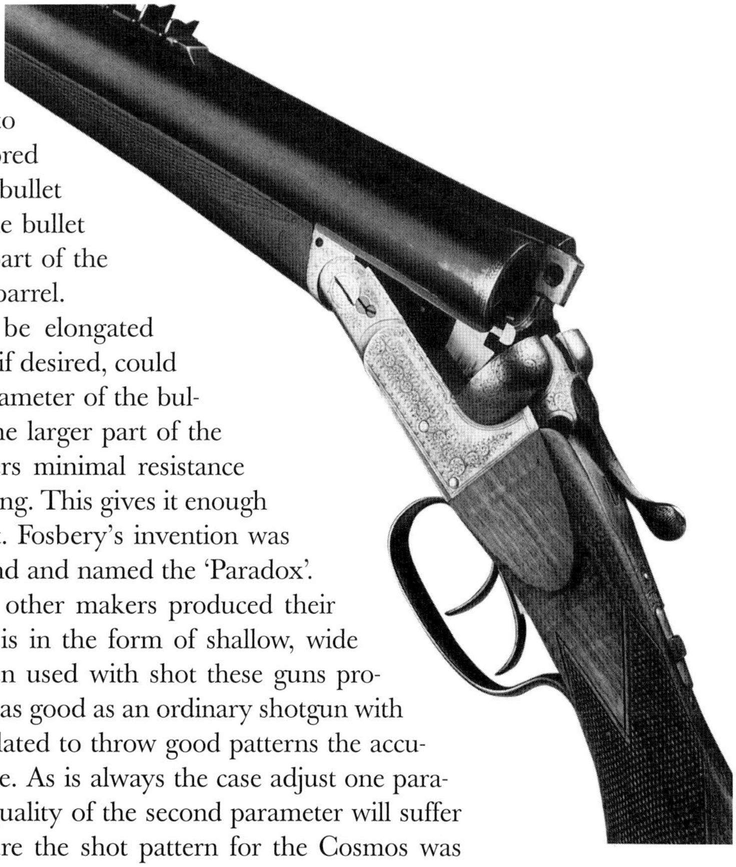

the best results were to be obtained
by making each groove slightly deeper
near its driving edge or side, i.e. the edge
or side that imparts the rotary impulse to
the bullet. As a result, when a choke bored
gun rifled in this way is used to fire a bullet
which fits the larger part of the barrel, the bullet
will be slightly compressed in the rifled part of the
barrel and will be rotated as it leaves the barrel.

It was recommended that the bullets be elongated
with one or more annular grooves, which if desired, could
be filled with lubricant. The maximum diameter of the bullet should be equal, or nearly equal, to the larger part of the
barrel so that when fired, the bullet offers minimal resistance
until the forcing cone aligns it with the rifling. This gives it enough
spin to ensure straight and accurate flight. Fosbery's invention was
first adopted in 1886 by Holland & Holland and named the 'Paradox'.
The patent expired in 1899, after which other makers produced their
own versions. In the Cosmos the rifling is in the form of shallow, wide
grooves without any sharp corners. When used with shot these guns produced acceptable patterns, although never as good as an ordinary shotgun with
regulated chokes. If the chokes were regulated to throw good patterns the accuracy of the gun as a rifle would deteriorate. As is always the case adjust one parameter to make an improvement and the quality of the second parameter will suffer
accordingly. In the contemporary literature the shot pattern for the Cosmos was
reported to be that of improved cylinder. In the Cogswell & Harrison catalogue of
1900 the average pattern with both barrels for 2 oz of No. 4 shot was reported as
193 pellets in a 36 inch circle. Since most customers required their guns predomi-
nantly for use with a solid projectile, it was this characteristic of their performance
which was optimised so as to ensure the best groupings, whilst their patterns as shotguns were generally regarded as less significant.

The example illustrated was donated to the company by a retired Colonel who
had used the gun extensively whilst serving overseas. The gun had been in his family for 80 years. His uncle, with whom he had used it to shoot snipe in India during
the Second World War had given it to him. While in Kashmir, the Colonel shot a
black bear with the gun after being prevailed upon by villagers frightened by the
bear's night-time raids. From 1955-58 he had used it for snipe shooting in Malaya
and, until his retirement in the 1970s, for game shooting at the Royal Military
College of Science shoot at Shrivenham and at the Royal School of Military
Engineering at Chatham. As the history of this gun demonstrates, it was an interesting compromise, between the quality of the pattern with No. 9 shot for snipe and
the accuracy of a solid bullet against an angry black bear. The Cosmos continued to
be advertised by the company until the beginning of the 1950s.

Cosmos ball and shot-
gun No. 42,975. This
can also be seen on
Plate 9.

Photo: David Grant

## Rook or Rabbit Rifles

Designed for shooting small game, the rook and rabbit rifle was a single barrel, low velocity lightly loaded weapon accurate up to around 70 yards. The calibre varied but was typically narrow bore. The muzzle loaders never usually exceeded 70-bore or .40 and the breech loading varieties ranged from .380 long, through .360, .320 long, .300 rook, .295 down to .255 and .250. A typical rook rifle had a short octagonal barrel, frequently referred to in the London trade as a 'threepenny piece' barrel (a misnomer since the threepenny piece had twelve sides), shallow rifled with a slow twist. Most were built on a drop-down breech loading action in a variety of hammer, semi-hammer or hammerless designs. Sights were usually restricted to a simple blade foresight and a fixed 'V' backsight, but were extremely accurate over the short ranges for which they were intended.

These little guns were of comparatively high quality, often being made in best grade by many of the established London makers including Holland & Holland, Purdey and Rigby. Cogswell & Harrison were no exception, offering hammerless top lever and side lever ejector models in a range of calibres from .22 up to .380. Up to the 1920s the company offered such rifles in both .300 and .250. The company's 1900 catalogue advertises a bolt action Certus rook and rabbit rifle available in .295 and .250 calibre. The better quality rook rifles remain popular with collectors, but the absence of ammunition following the Second World War meant that they were abandoned in favour of the .22 rimfire and those that survived were sometimes bored out to .410 shotguns.

.295 sidelever self-ejecting Rook Rifle, No. 17,154, completed in April 1899; it weighs 5 lb 2 oz.

Photo: David Grant

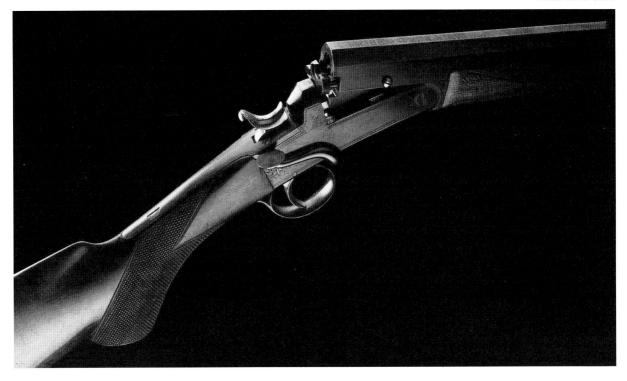

# 17  Master Eye

Edgar Harrison wrote in *A Dissertation Upon Guns and Shooting*:

> One almost needs to apologise to the reader for introducing the well-worn topic of the master eye, but the excuse for its insertion must be that without it a book on shooting would be incomplete.

The problem was, and still is, what to do if an individual wants to fire a gun from one shoulder, but aiming is controlled by the opposite eye. A modern philosophy is that a right-handed shooter with a left master eye (by far the commonest problem) should either learn to control their vision by dimming the left eye just before taking the shot, or, ideally learn to shoot from the left shoulder with an appropriately fitted gun where the stock is cast-on to align the rib with the dominant eye. The general convention is that right-handed shooters with a right master eye will require some cast-off and left-handed shooters with a left master eye some cast-on (a stock angled to the right is described as being 'cast-off' and a stock angled to the left as 'cast-on').

Gunmakers like Cogswell & Harrison and others addressed the problem in a more direct manner. Their solution was simply to fit the gun with a stock that allowed the shooter to align the rib of the gun with their master eye regardless of which shoulder they shot from. This solution gave rise to what many modern sportsmen and women think of as a most peculiar contrivance, the cross-over or cross-eyed stock. These unusual stocks allow shooting left-eyed from the right shoulder and vice versa.

Semi cross-eyed stocks where the degree of cast is less severe were also employed for those shooters who did not require a fully cross-eyed stock, but because one eye was considerably stronger required more cast than normal. Shooters having central vision also used semi-cross-eyed stocks. Cogswell & Harrison offered cross-eyed and semi-cross-eyed stocks as an option across their complete range of shotguns.

Details extracted from the company records show that Cogswell & Harrison shotgun serial No. 45,450 (illustrated on page 107), was completed on 12 August 1914 as a 'K' quality 12-bore boxlock hammerless ejector on an Avant Tout type action fitted with an assisted opening mechanism. The 30 in. barrels were bored with six points of choke in the right barrel and 20 points in the left barrel. The barrels were nitroproofed for $1^1/8$ oz of shot and, when struck up and fitted to the action, weighed 3 lb 3 oz. The finished and assembled gun weighed 6 lb $11^1/2$ oz. The records completely describe the 'cross-eyed' stock giving the length, bends and casts which were customised for the first owner.

With a cross-eyed stock it was not sufficient just to have complicated woodwork cut to the shape required to align the gun with the dominant eye. It was often necessary on those guns requiring a large degree of cast for the locks and metal work at the rear of the action to be modified. They had to follow the bend in the head of the stock, so the top strap and lever, the safety mechanism, trigger plate and guard were all built accordingly.

There has often been debate over how well a gun with a cross-eyed stock shoots. Gough Thomas reported that cast-off in a normal side-by-side gun, i.e. right-handed

(above) John Peskett, inventor of the Cogswell & Harrison eye corrector. (below) diagram showing correct and incorrect barrel alignment.

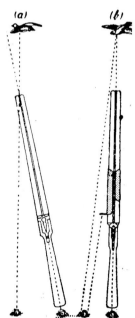

(a) Incorrect alignment—left eye master.
(b) Correct alignment by using the Eye Corrector. The left eye, though master, is blocked out from aligning gun—object can, however, be seen with both eyes.

*Incorrect and correct*

grip with a right master eye, tended to produce a slight lateral error in the left barrel. He then revisited this idea in view of guns fitted with cross-eyed stocks where the degree of cast-off by far exceeds that of a normal gun. If the normal cast-off of $1/2$ in. produces a measurable lateral error why doesn't a gun where the cast-off can be in the order of several inches give an enormous lateral error? He concludes that the springing of the wood in the hand portion of the stock, produced in reaction to the forces of recoil, compensates for any lateral error in the barrels, which would be expected to shoot in the opposite direction to the cast.

Owners of guns fitted with cross-eyed stocks do however need to be very careful in their choice of cartridge. For reasons of comfort and accuracy, heavy loads are best avoided since the axis of recoil is offset several inches from the stock.

There were a number of alternatives to the cross-over stock on offer from the ever imaginative gunmakers, the majority of which did not require such elaborate and extensive modifications. One example was the Monopeian sight described by W. W. Greener in his book *Modern Shot Guns* published in 1888. The Monopeian sight was the invention of the Reverend E. Elmhurst and appears to have been an ingenious solution to the problem encountered by sportsmen who had lost the sight of one eye. Here the re-alignment of the dominant eye with the target is not achieved by bending the stock across the face but by bringing the foresight out to one side of the muzzle and fitting an additional sight at or near the breech end of the barrels. Both sights were carried on outriggers about an inch in length brazed to the barrels. There is no doubt that sights such as these proved effective with practice and also overcame the difficulties of firing a gun with a stock bent across the shooter's face. Needless to say sights mounted on outriggers are very vulnerable and easily broken.

Another solution to the problem lay in blocking the vision of the dominant eye by means of a correcting device which obscured the target from view, enabling the weaker eye to be in sole control of the direction in which the gun was being pointed. These devices were collectively known as Correctors or Obliterators and were fixed either to the barrels like the Monopeian sights or attached to removable hand guards of the type still popular with some shooters.

One such example was the subject of Patent No. 53 of 1884 awarded to Thomas Gilbert of 54 Great Marlborough Street, London. The Gilbert Shooting Corrector was a rectangular metal plate fitted to the upper left-hand side of the gun barrel by means of a threaded screw, which located with a fastening soldered to the breech end of the barrels. This device allowed the weaker eye to see the rib and the fore sight with both eyes open, something which previously had required the left eye to be closed, thereby reducing considerably the field of view. It was this drawback that all the sight correctors and obliterators sought to rectify whilst transferring control to the weaker eye.

Closing one eye not only restricts what the shooter can see but also limits the estimation of range, which in order to be accurate requires binocular vision. Later the solutions became somewhat simpler and less permanent with the introduction of sight correctors that were not fixed to the barrels. Patent No. 4,226 of 1885 to W. W. Watts, was simply a ring worn on the thumb of the left hand to which was attached a disc to obscure the vision of the left eye. The 'thumbstall' method attributed to Robert Churchill was a simpler and even cheaper alternative. This was the practice of raising the thumb of the hand supporting the forend to obscure the vision of the dominant eye. Wearing a cap with its peak or brim pulled down to partially obscure the view is a similar alternative to a mechanical device.

Generally, obliterators were the preferred method and came in numerous styles and shapes, either fixed to the barrels or held in position by means of clips, guards or elastic bands. Cogswell & Harrison offered the troubled sportsman an affordable alternative solution in the form of the Cogswell & Harrison Eye Corrector or Obliterator. The device was designed by John Peskett, shooting instructor and gun fitter at Cogswell & Harrison's shooting school, who later became a member of the board and then in 1933 a director of the company.

The Obliterator consisted of a leather-covered steel hand-guard, which slips on the barrels over the muzzle. One side of the hand-guard is extended back towards the breech end of the barrels and the end is turned outwards to form a disc, which protrudes from the barrels and obscures the view of the muzzles. In this way the dominant left eye is prevented from seeing the muzzle of the gun and controlling alignment with the target. The obliterator was available in right- and left-handed models: the right-handed model had the disc fitted to the left side to obscure the view of the left eye and the left-handed model had the disc fitted to the right side.

Eye corrector and cross over stock. One problem, two solutions.

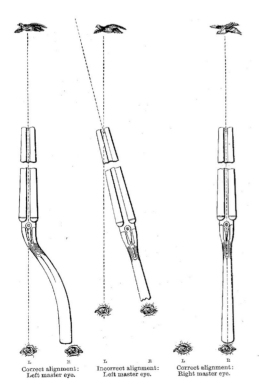

Correct alignment: Left master eye.    Incorrect alignment: Left master eye.    Correct alignment: Right master eye.

From *Shooting, with Game and Gun Room Notes*, by 'Blagdon'.

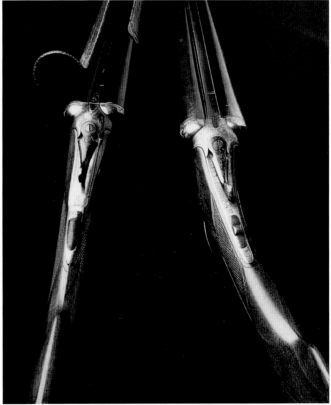

Photo: Ann Bolton

## 18  Contribution to Clay Pigeon Shooting

The sport of clay pigeon shooting in its many manifestations has its foundations in the sport of live pigeon shooting. This became popular as a competitive sport during the nineteenth century in and around London at gun clubs such as Hornsey Wood and The London Gun Club, Notting Hill. The birds were released from collapsing boxes known as traps, the trap operator releasing the bird by pulling on a cord; a no-bird was one that did not fly when the trap was pulled. These boxes were in front of the shooter whose position was decided on a handicap basis. Despite its somewhat dubious sporting credentials, live pigeon shooting contributed many terms which persist today in clay pigeon shooting where every clay pigeon shooter is familiar with the terms trap, pull and no-bird. As live pigeon shooting grew in popularity it soon spread throughout the British Empire, Europe and into North and South America. Competitions attracted large crowds and considerable prize money could be at stake and the individual competitors often wagered large sums on the outcome.

The widespread interest in competitive shooting during the first quarter of the nineteenth century led to a search for an artificial target with which to replace the live bird. Among the first attempts was the glass ball target first seen in England in the 1830s but according to some sources it was introduced by Charles Portlock of Boston in 1836. At first the balls were made of smooth colourless glass about $2^1/_2$ in. in diameter; later amber or blue glass was used to make them more visible and the surfaces often had thin ribs cast into them to prevent the shot from glancing off and to make the balls break more easily, an idea protected by US Patent No. 188,334. Perhaps the zenith of the glass ball target came when they were filled with feathers to make it easier to judge when hit. The traps to throw the glass ball targets were ingenious affairs and were often named after famous shooters of the time; the varieties available included a catapult type known as the 'Bogardus' which used a flat coach spring to provide the impetus to the target and a number of revolving types such as the 'Carver' and the 'Card' which used coil springs to project the targets.

The Bogardus trap was named after Adam Bogardus of Elkhart, Illinois, a professional shotgunner and Pigeon Champion of the World, who on 10 April 1877 was successful in filing US Patent 188,334 for the ribbed glass ball target. Bogardus was a gifted shot and started his shooting career as a hunter. In 1884 he became part of Buffalo Bill Cody's Wild West Show until in the December of the same year he lost all his gear in a steamboat collision on the Mississippi river. Bogardus's fate did not improve for he left the Wild West Show in an attempt to make a legal claim against the boat owners and was replaced by a young vaudeville star by the name of Annie Oakley.

Bogardus's fame was made in the arena of inanimate target shooting and specifically the glass ball. On 4 July 1879 he attempted the feat of breaking 5,000 glass balls in 500 minutes, which he achieved with 20 minutes to spare; the following year he broke 6,000 glass balls in the same time. Glass balls were not entirely satisfactory as a target since they could be highly inconsistent: they often broke on throwing, sometimes they would not break when hit and the debris created was dangerous to both man and beast. The major downfall however, was that the flight of the glass ball was inferior to that of a live pigeon. These poor flight characteristics presented the shooter with an easy target; consequently scores of 100% even for sportsman of moderate skill were not uncommon. The ultimate demise of the glass ball target however, came with the introduction of the first clay pigeon or disc target.

The development of the clay pigeon is generally attributed to George Ligowsky of Cincinnati in the early 1880s, but around the same time an Englishman named McCaskey produced a similar design. The Ligowsky clay pigeon was a moulded clay saucer to which a paper tongue was attached, the saucer being held by the tongue in the clamp of the trap. The flight of the target was uniform and more truly resembled that of a pigeon. However, the clay was kiln-fired to produce a terracotta ceramic similar to a plant pot and sometimes the targets were so hard that they would not break when hit.

One ingenious solution to the problem of unbreakable targets and pieces of broken clay littering the countryside, was the brass pigeon made by Kynoch & Co. These re-useable targets were stamped from sheet brass and had a cardboard base fixed to the rim. The targets were filled with fine charcoal and produced a cloud of dust when hit. Further improvement in the clay pigeon came with the formulation of targets made from mixtures of ash, pitch, resin and water cast in a mould.

In 1875 the Ranelagh Club in London was the first shooting ground in England to offer inanimate targets. *The Illustrated London News* of 10 March 1883 reported a 'Terracotta Pigeon' shooting demonstration held at the Ranelagh Club and in 1893 the Inanimate Bird Shooting Society held its first championship in Wimbledon Park. This Society, with the support of Eley-Kynoch, later became the Clay Pigeon Shooting Association.

Perhaps the most significant breakthrough came in 1888 when Cogswell & Harrison introduced the 'Swiftsure' trap and targets in which pitch was substituted for the clay. The Swiftsure traps were available as both single and double rise and became very popular with the clubs offering the new sport of clay pigeon shooting. A meeting of the London Gun Club was called on 28 March 1889 to assess the Swiftsure trap. Following this, the Inanimate Bird Shooting Association authorised its use for all their competitions. An upgraded model introduced in 1894 retailed for £1 12s 6d with the double trap at £2 4s 6d. The clay pigeons cost 4s 6d per 100.

By the close of the nineteenth century, the shooting of live birds released from traps was under increasing pressure from public opinion and it was doomed in England and much of the Empire.

The Swiftsure clay pigeon trap authorised by the Inanimate Bird Shooting Association (later to become the CPSA) in 1889 for use in all its competitions.

"SWIFTSURE"

## Traps and Birds.

*(REGISTERED).*

Introduced in 1888.
The Leading Trap ever since
Used by
Home and Colonial Clubs.

*One Quality only—*
"THE BEST."

"SWIFTSURE"
(REG?)

### TRAPS.
SIMPLICITY OF MECHANISM.

| | | | |
|---|---|---|---|
| Finest Extant, Single ... ... ... | Cash | 25/- |
| Improved Model Ditto ... ... ... | " | 35/- |
| Double Rise Ditto ... ... ... | " | 52/6 |

Accessories for Fixing, &c., extra on Single Rise 5/-,
Double Rise, 7/- cash.

**BIRDS.** — SWIFTSURES are the Standard Birds for best quality in the Market. Travel well. Fly well. Break well.
Per 500 Barrel, cash 15/-.          Per 100 Box, cash, 5/-.

OFFICIAL RULES AND SCORE BOOK POST FREE ON APPLICATION.

"Swiftsure" Traps and Birds can be obtained from all Gunmakers and Dealers.

K

Charles Dickens mirrors the feelings of much of Victorian society in his book *Martin Chuzzlewit*, published in 1865, in which one of the characters, Poll Sweedlepipe, supplies sparrows for shooting matches. The sport was outlawed in various North American states at the turn of the century and in Britain it was effectively abolished in 1910, reportedly at the insistence of Queen Alexandra and was finally banned by Parliament with the Captive Birds (Prohibition of Shooting) Act of 1921.

Many top English gunmakers built specialist pigeon guns and widely advertised the competitions won using their guns. Cogswell & Harrison was no exception. Despite the repulsion felt today for competitive live pigeon shooting, it led, as has been said, directly to clay pigeon shooting and the gunmakers who made pigeon guns laid the foundations for modern competition guns. Down-the-line trap shooting, for example, has similarities to live bird shooting. The shooter stands at a mark a set distance behind five traps positioned approximately 5 yards apart. One major difference was that with live birds the gun was held with the stock below the shoulder as in sporting shooting and FITASC. There was also a double rise variation where two traps were simultaneously pulled.

The pigeon gun was very different from a game gun. It was stocked and ribbed to throw the centre of the shot pattern high of the point of aim. A heavy charge of powder and shot was the norm, typically 1¼ oz and a heavy gun was required to absorb the repeated recoil and to promote a steady stance. Typically, a 12-bore gun chambered for a 2¾ in. cartridge shooting 1¼ oz of shot would weigh around 7½ lb. This was later limited under competition rules to a maximum of 8 lb.

The principal requirement was for the gun to be able to shoot a heavy charge at high velocity and achieve the penetration necessary to bring down the rapidly retreating target. A shot charge of 1¼ oz represented an increase of approximately 30 to 50 pellets over a contemporary game load, but nonetheless, great care was taken to ensure the guns shot regular and even patterns. With the advent of choke boring in the 1870s the barrels were choke regulated, typically to ¾ or full choke. Modern pigeon shooters often assert that the best gun for shooting wild pigeons over decoys is a tightly choked trap gun.

Cogswell & Harrison's Grand Prix Pigeon gun was sold as a specialist gun for live pigeon shooting with great emphasis being placed upon the regular patterns. The company's catalogue of 1900 proudly states: '. . . the utmost care and attention being paid to the boring and shooting, the patterns obtained being very regular, like "rain falling on the pavement" . . .'. These guns were built both on the best quality Victor sidelock action and in a boxlock version.

The example illustrated on Plate 8, Grand Prix Pigeon Gun No. 40,521, was one of three guns built to the same specification and completed in 1906. The whereabouts of the two other guns, Nos. 40,519 and 40,520 is unknown. No. 40,521 was built on a type T108 12-bore deluxe, assisted opening box lock ejector action fitted with ornamental sideplates. The action was fitted with a non-automatic safety, double triggers and was decorated with bold scrollwork throughout. The lock up between the barrels and action was extremely tight, with the addition of a Greener type cross-bolt which in operation reinforces both the bar of the action and the under barrel bolt. Side clips were also included to improve the lateral rigidity of the gun. The 30 in. barrels were of fine 'Arcus' steel with 2¾ in. chambers and were proofed for 1¼ oz of shot. The right and left barrels were choke regulated at 31 and 32 points respectively, i.e. approximately ¾ choke in each.

It is interesting to note that when this gun was made, the choke in each barrel was expressed as the actual amount of constriction, measured in thousands of an inch or 'points'. The barrels were regulated for No. 6 shot with the right barrel placing an average of 223 pellets into a 30 in. circle at 40 yd and the left barrel 226 pellets. Compare these figures to those in the published tables for a charge of $1\frac{1}{4}$ oz of No. 6 shot: $\frac{3}{4}$ choke at 40 yards puts 219 pellets into a 30 in. circle and full choke 236 pellets into the same diameter circle. The rib was a file cut flat rib and the barrels when struck up weighed 3 lb 10 oz. The stock measures $14\frac{1}{2}$ in. from the front trigger to the toe and has a bend at the comb of $1\frac{7}{16}$ and 2 in. at the heel. When completed the gun weighed 7 lb 6 oz.

It is interesting to compare the features of this gun with those of a modern clay pigeon gun built for trap shooting. The modern trap gun is almost exclusively a 12-bore over-and-under with $2\frac{3}{4}$ in. chambers firing a $1\frac{1}{8}$ oz (32 gram) or 1 oz (28 gram) load. The trap gun usually has 30 in. choked barrels (although 32 in. barrels are gaining in popularity) and for protection against the repeated recoil it will be of full weight, typically $7\frac{1}{2}$ to $8\frac{1}{4}$ lb.

One advantage claimed for the over-and-under is that it delivers the second or top barrel pattern a little higher than that of the first or bottom barrel, 6 to 9 in. is typical. The advantage of this arrangement is that for second barrel shots at rising targets the high delivering second barrel may compensate for a natural tendency to shoot low with the second shot. As the trap gun is shouldered prior to calling for the target, the trap stock is longer and straighter than that of a game gun. The comb of the stock is high and level allowing accurate alignment of the shooter's aiming eye

---

## The 2 in.12-Bore

Although the Cogswell & Harrison $27\frac{1}{2}$ in. barrelled guns were lighter 12-bores, the true 12-bore light-weight was the 2 in. chambered gun. The 2 in. 12-bore and the issues surrounding its use, manufacturing and proofing are interestingly discussed in Douglas Tate's The Birmingham Gunmakers.

Stated briefly, the 2 in. cartridge shoots a load of $\frac{3}{4}$ oz of shot. Given the gunmakers' rule of thumb ratio that the gun weight to shot load should be at least 96, it will be seen that a 12-bore weighing somewhat less than 6 lb would result. This is essentially a 12-bore shooting a 20-bore load in a gun which would weigh about the same as a 20-bore. However, its light weight is not the only advantage. The $\frac{3}{4}$ oz of shot in a 12-bore barrel results in a length of shot column which is roughly the same as the barrel diameter, i.e. about $\frac{3}{4}$ in. This is about ideal and produces quite exceptionally good patterns.

These lightweight guns found greatest favour during the 1930s and most were manufactured at that time. To meet this demand, Cogswell & Harrison introduced a new range of guns, 'The 12 minor', in 1934. The guns were based on the existing models but had 2 in. chambers to shoot a load of $\frac{3}{4}$ oz. The

barrels ranged from 25 to $27\frac{1}{2}$ in. and the guns weighed around 5 lb 4 oz to 5 lb 6 oz depending on barrel length. They were offered in three side-lock versions: the Victor at 100 guineas, the Primic at 80 guineas and the Crown at 50 guineas. The Konor, a sideplated boxlock, was offered at 40 guineas.

The catalogue described these guns as 'the lightest of the light' and at the same time advertised its '12 minor' cartridges. These 2 in. cartridges with $\frac{3}{4}$ oz of shot were sold at 13s 6d per hundred with 'carriage paid on 500 lots to any railway station in Great Britain'. This was in the mid 1930s when 2 in. 12-bores were experiencing niche popularity.

However, Cogswell & Harrison continued to offer 2 in. guns much later. Thus an advertisement in the 28 July 1977 issue of the Shooting Times offered the 12-bore Victor sidelock ejector with $2\frac{3}{4}$, $2\frac{1}{2}$ or 2 in. chambers. This model with detachable locks cost at that time around £3,500.

The 2 in. chambered gun appears to be experiencing somewhat of a revival, particularly in the United States.

with the rib of the gun which can be raised, knurled to cut down reflection and is often fitted with a mid-sight in addition to the foresight.

The fitting of a mid-sight provides the shooter with a sight picture where they see the front sight sat on the top of the intermediate sight in a figure-of-eight configuration. This sight picture requires a high comb and assists the shooter in placing the shot pattern high of the rising and retreating target. In combination, the figure-of-eight sight picture and the high comb allow the shooter to sit the target on the front sight prior to firing.

The Grand Prix Pigeon Gun is a classic example of the forerunner to the modern trap gun and as such a number of direct comparisons with a modern gun can be made. Although a side-by-side, the length of the barrels are very much standard for a trap gun with this length helping to promote a steady swing. The flat file cut rib is also typical of a modern competition gun with the machined surface reducing reflection and aiding concentration.

The degree of choking required for the trap disciplines is open to some debate with many factors influencing the choice. Many fixed choke trap guns are supplied with ³/₄ and full choke. Some people regard ³/₄ as a little tight for the first barrel and would favour ¹/₂ choke. However, unless the shooter is an extremely fast shot, full choke remains standard for the second barrel. Modern multichoke guns allow the shooter to experiment with degrees of choking depending upon their individual style and the variety of the trap discipline (DTL, Double Rise, ABT, Universal Trap etc.). The choice of ³/₄ and ³/₄ may be a little puzzling for a trap type discipline but in live pigeon shooting the targets were not simply inanimate discs of powdered limestone and bitumen thrown on a defined trajectory, but live quarry which presented the shooter with a variety of angles and speeds.

The stock dimensions are very familiar to those people who regularly shoot the trap disciplines, although at 14¹/₂ in. many may regard the length as a little on the short side for a style of shooting where the gun is pre-mounted before calling for the target but in live pigeon shooting the gun was held below the shoulder before calling for the trap to be pulled. Extra length helps to control any erratic movement in the gun and with the trap disciplines, smooth and consistent gun movement is very important.

From the French Catalogue of 1909.

Plate 15  The locks of a new Cogswell & Harrison Best London self-opening SLE.

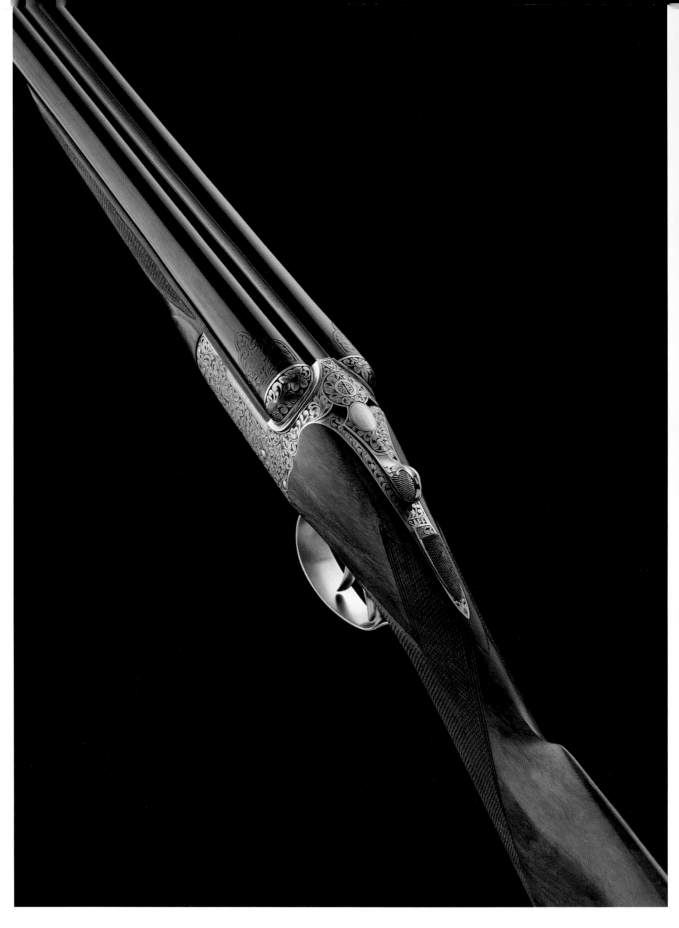

Plate 16  An Extra Quality Victoria (special) 20-bore BLE with round body, chopperlump barrels, intercepting sears and removable crosspin. These are current and may be ordered in all calibres. *(Courtesy A.J. Bird.)*

The stock is fitted with a semi-pistol grip, which is somewhat unusual for a gun fitted with double triggers since a straight stock allows the hand to move back and bring the trigger finger onto the rear trigger for the second shot. A possible explanation may be that the semi-pistol grip contributed to a more stable shooting stance and helped maintain consistent hand position. The non-automatic safety was also used to assist in maintaining a consistent shooting position and rapid target acquisition since no movement of either the head or the hand was required to move the safety into the firing position. Perhaps more importantly, a non-automatic safety removed the danger of a missed target due to the safety being left on; the significance of a missed target is even more apparent when one considers the money from prizes and personal wagers that were at stake.

Single selective triggers are today fitted as standard on most competition guns but when the Grand Prix was built single triggers, both non-selective and fully selective, were an option. The advantage of a single trigger over a double trigger is that the shooter does not have to move their grip on the stock between shooting the first and the second barrel, thereby enabling aimed shots to be taken more quickly. The early non-selective single triggers were at their best on a pigeon gun where the more open barrel was fired first as a matter of course. In Cogswell & Harrison's catalogue of 1900 the single trigger is offered as an extra for the Grand Prix at a premium of 2 Guineas and in the same catalogue the selective version of the single trigger was advertised as costing an additional £1 1s over the price of the non-selective single trigger mechanism. Conversion to single trigger was offered at 6 guineas.

The Cogswell & Harrison single trigger was the subject of Patent No. 4,005 of 1895. A single trigger to operate two locks was not a new idea. The ingenuity came in designing and building a single-trigger mechanism that retained the feel and ease of pull of double triggers whilst preventing the involuntary pull that could result in a double discharge. It was from these early designs that the modern fully selective single-trigger mechanisms in use today evolved.

It is plain to see that the modern clay pigeon shooter, and in particular one whose chosen sport is trap shooting, owes a huge debt to the master gunmakers without whose ingenuity and expertise the specialised modern shotgun may not have evolved. Despite the dubious origins of live pigeon shooting we cannot fail to recognise the contribution made by gunmakers like Cogswell & Harrison to the development of clay pigeon shooting as a highly competitive sport. Not only did Cogswell & Harrison lead the development of the shotgun with such innovations as a reliable single trigger mechanism, but it also helped pioneer the development and use of the inanimate target in the form of the clay pigeon.

# 19 Ammunition and Cartridges

Cogswell & Harrison were also innovative in the field of shotgun ammunition and the equipment used to manufacture and test it.

For cartridge loading, Cogswell & Harrison devised machinery to ensure regularity of the shot pattern. Powder and ammunition were tested with an electric chronograph, force gauge, cap tester and recoil gun. A secret waterproofing process was invented and carried out by selected women employees in a purpose built chamber. The turnover at the end of a cartridge was of particular importance and controlled by further apparatus. Barrels were built to register pressures, and an electric instrument devised to measure 'mean velocity' by the breaking of a wire at two points in the line of fire. The chronograph registered timing of shot between points, and the recoil gun checked recoil in relation to pressure. Finally, the caps were made to maintain the standard of the cartridge.

Cogswell & Harrison took their manufacturing of cartridges very seriously both in terms of the quality control procedures within the manufacturing process and the sheer volume of the activity. John Peskett gives a good sense of this in describing the Gillingham factory:

On the ground floor were the cartridge loading rooms in which several hundred girls

Advertisements for the company's range of cartridges including the Blagdon which was reintroduced in 1994.

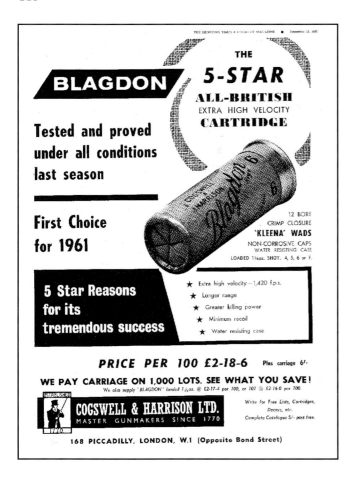

(above) Advertisement for the Bladgon cartridge from *The Field*, February 1956

(left) Advertisement for Blagdon cartridges from *Shooting Times*, January 1961.

rolled paper tubes for cartridge making. Also made there were the components such as the caps and wadding and there was of course the final assembly. Another section housed presses for the production of metallic cartridges. At right angles to these rooms were the drying rooms, powder chamber. . .

The 'Victor' (following the name of the gun) was the top of the range cartridge, produced and sold for 10s 6d a hundred. The registered zig-zag markings became known in all sporting establishments at home and abroad. The list of trade names for the cartridges (see Appendix 3) gives some sense of the scale of the company's activities in the cartridge manufacturing and related gunpowder and explosive areas.

The company's deep involvement in the manufacture of ammunition inevitably led it to involvement in the development of powders and explosives. The making of a really reliable powder is a complicated task. Cogswell & Harrison obtained the finest scientific testing appliances and registered their own 'Vicmos' gunpowder. The development of a smokeless powder became desirable as it reduced noise and recoil. However, black powder was more reliable. The Schultze Gunpowder Company was the first to manufacture a successful nitro-powder and Cogswell & Harrison combined with them in the early 1900s to produce a powder known as 'Cogschultze'. In 1900 Cogswell & Harrison registered 'Fusilite', then the 'Kelor' and 'Markoroid' explosive substances in 1907 and 1908. Registered names of cartridges such as 'Bono', 'Farmo', 'Molto', 'Westro' and 'Pluvoid' were marketed and enjoyed a good reputation at home and abroad.

Manufacture ceased. One reason for this was that a large combine entered into competition with Cogswell & Harrison but the main reason was the death, in 1915, of Edgar Harrison's only son Cogswell, the manager of the Colnbrook business. He was tragically killed at the age of 23 in an explosion at the Powder Mills at Colnbrook in which three other members of the staff also lost their lives. Cogswell Harrison was the sole heir and it was intended that he would succeed his father. A distressed Edgar Harrison disposed of all the Colnbrook property and closed down the shooting school.

It is clear in retrospect that the developments in cartridge making and smokeless power by the company could well have led to the equivalent of a Fiocchi or a Rotweil. Competition undoubtedly contributed to the end of this activity, but the death of Cogswell Harrison had a major and significant impact. This great tragedy for Cogswell & Harrison was a decisive factor in its cessation of gunpowder manufacture.

## A Sweet Shooting Gun

Throughout the company records, certainly those of the past 100 years, there has been a fairly consistent ratio of gun weight to the cartridge charge. This remains true whether the gun in question is a small-, twelve- or large-bore gun for a special purpose such as wildfowling.

*The light gun needs a light load* - Burrard

The ratio gun weight to weight of shot charge is one of the key factors affecting a gun's recoil. There are of course other factors such as the user's sensitivity to recoil, the fit of the gun and the user's physique. Years of practical experience in the field has demonstrated that other things being equal, there is a weight of gun with which one can generally shoot a given charge with comfort. Readers who wish to deal with this question in a scientific and technical sense should refer to Burrard's The *Modern Shotgun* Volume 1 or Gough Thomas's *Shotguns and Cartridges*.

Two forms of recoil are significant, the sensible recoil as described above and the dynamic recoil.

Assuming that the gun in question is a traditional British game gun, with no recoil-operated parts as in autoloaders, or no muzzle brakes, then the momentum of the recoiling gun is equal to the momentum of the charge. Since momentum is weight x velocity, it follows that the velocity of recoil is the weight of shot charge x its velocity ÷ weight of gun. If the weight of the shot charge and its velocity are fixed - that is to say there is a chosen cartridge, the gun's dynamic recoil will be determined by its weight.

Burrard suggests that the velocity of recoil should be kept to 16 ft/sec. It follows from this that the weight of the gun should be about 96 times the weight of the shot charge. This confirms what long experience has shown, that broadly, a gun should weigh 6 lb for each ounce of shot. Thus the gunmakers' rule of thumb ratio, gun weight to shot load equals 96 is roughly the ratio to be found throughout the Cogswell & Harrison records!

As a staff member put it when describing the advantages of this ratio: 'A sweet shooting gun, easy on the shoulder and light enough to carry all day'.

# And the Future?

W e have attempted to encapsulate 223 years of turbulent company history into about 120 pages. Such compression inevitably means that some topics could benefit from even further research. However, what clearly emerges above all the detail is that Cogswell & Harrison has always displayed resilience, tenacity and inge- nuity. These qualities inspire the current owners and instil a sense of responsibility toward those who have nurtured such a heritage. They are also proving to be a source of inspiration to all those currently involved in the company.

As we enter the twenty-first century with its hurricane of technological and social change it is reassuring for Cogswell & Harrison owners worldwide to know that 'their gunmaker' is alive and well and producing and restoring fine sporting guns. Indeed, it is a sign of the times that current information can be accessed on the Cogswell & Harrison website: www.cogswell.co.uk and that anyone can make enquiries via the e-mail address: info@cogswell.co.uk. Just call, click or fax!

The Cogswell & Harrison trade label, 1993 to the present.

# Appendix 1: Cogswell & Harrison Addresses and Business Names/Activities

| DATES | LOCATION | BUSINESS |
|---|---|---|
| 1770 - 1842 | 4, Bengal Place, London | B. Cogswell, Gunmaker, Pawnbroker, Repository of guns and pistols |
| 1794 - 1804 | 224 Strand, London | Hector Essex (relative of Cogswell), Manufacturer of Hardware |
| 1805 - 1820 | 104 and 223-4 Strand, London | Hector Essex, Gunsmith and Jeweller |
| 1821 - 1833 | 224 Strand, London | Robert Essex (relative of Cogswell), Silversmith and dealer in Firearms |
| 1835 - 1841 | 224 Strand, London | Edward Benton, Firearms Dealer and Silversmith |
| 1842 - 1856 | 224 Strand, London | B. Cogswell (successor to E. Benton), Gun and Pistol Warehouse, Gunmaker |
| 1857 - 1863 | 224 Strand, London | Benjamin Cogswell, Gunmaker |
| 1863 - 1879 | 223-224 Strand, London | Cogswell & Harrison, Gunmakers |
| 1880 - 1897 | 142 New Bond Street, London | Cogwell & Harrison, Gunmakers |
| 1882 - 1928 | 226 Strand, London | Cogswell & Harrison, Gunmakers |
| 1886 - 1894 | Ferndale Estate, Harrow, Middx | Factory. Gun and rifle manufacture |
| 1886 - 1915 | Colnbrook, near Windsor | Shooting School, Works and Powder Mill |
| 1889 - 1905 | Malden, Surrey | Blagdon Shooting School and works |
| 1893 - 1922 | Gillingham Street, Victoria, London | Factory, Laboratories, Indoor Shooting Range |
| 1897 - 1917 | 141 New Bond Street, London | Cogswell & Harrison, Gunmakers |
| 1901 - 1936 | 26 Avenue de l'Opéra, Paris | Showrooms, Retail Depot, Associated Shooting Park |
| 1908 - 1909 | Craven Street, Strand, London | Wm Moore & Grey (in acquisition by C & H) |
| 1917 - 1982 | 168 Piccadilly, London | Showroom, Main London Establishment |
| 1922 - 1932 | Feltham, Middlesex | Small Arms Factory |
| 1927 - 1934 | 94 Queen Street, Exeter | Shop and Retail Depot |
| 1935 - 1957 | 21 Park Road East, Acton, London W3 | Factory; Rifle and gun manufacturing; Precision engineering; Contractor to Ministry of Supply, War Office, Admiralty etc. |
| 1957 to 1963 | Bollo Lane, Acton, London | International Armament Corporation of America and Canada (later Interarmco) |
| 1963 - 1965 | Connaught Street, London | Workshop |
| 1965 - 1969 | 91/93 Lots Road, Chelsea, London SW10 | Factory, Blanch & Co., tenants of C & H for a short time |
| 1983 to 1993 | Farlows, Pall Mall, London | Cogswell & Harrison |
| 1984 - 1989 | 5 King Street London 66 Great Suffolk Street, London | Gunmaking Licence to J. Roberts & Son |
| 1993 to Present | Heathcliffe, Parkers Lane, Maidens Green, Berks, RG42 6LE | Workshop and sales |
| 1993 to Present | Thatcham House, 95 Sussex Place, Slough, Berks, SL1 1NN | Head Office (information, archives, accounts) Tel: 01753 520866  Fax: 01753 575770 |

Note: Overlapping dates indicate two or more locations in simultaneous use.

# Appendix 2: Patents

| Date | | | Number | Inventor(s) | Invention | Notes |
|---|---|---|---|---|---|---|
| Application | Specification | Accepted | | | | |
| **1864**<br>26 July | 1 Feb | 10 May | 271 | **Edward Harrison**<br>The Strand, Middlesex | *Improvements in Breech-loading Firearms*<br><br>Cocking (pinfire) | Agent: William Spence<br>50 Chancery Lane<br><br>Illustrated |
| **1880**<br>22 Jan | This invention received provisional protection only | | 278 | **Edward Harrison**<br>The Strand, Middlesex &<br>**Thomas Southgate**<br>Burton Crescent, London | *Improvements in Breech-loading Firearms*<br><br>Cocking (pinfire) | Not illustrated |
| **1883**<br>14 April | 13 Oct | | 1,903 | **Edward Harrison**<br>The Strand, Middlesex &<br>**Frederick Beesley**<br>Edgware Road | *Improvements in Breech-loading Firearms*<br><br>Cocking (hammerless) | Illustrated |
| **1884**<br>8 May | | | 7,437 | **E. Harrison** & **E. Harrison** | *Self-cocking break-down Firearms* | Abandoned Application Specification not printed |
| **1884**<br>18 Aug | 24 April | | 11,382 | **Edgar Harrison**<br>142 New Bond Street &<br>**Frederick Beesley**<br>85 Edgware Road | *An Intercepting Block Safety for Gun Locks*<br><br>Intercepting block safety mechanism | Illustrated |
| **1886**<br>29 Jan | 27 Oct | | 1,326 | **Edgar Harrison**<br>226 Strand &<br>**William Jackman Jeffrey**<br>55 Britannia Rd, Fulham | *Improvements in Combined Sight Elevators and Windgauges*<br><br>Vernier gauge for rearsight | Illustrated |
| **1886**<br>25 May | 25 Feb | 25 March | 7,029 | **Edgar Harrison**<br>226 Strand &<br>**William Jackman Jeffrey**<br>55 Britannia Rd, Fulham | *Improvements in Foresight Protectors for Military and Other Rifles*<br><br>Foresight protector | Illustrated |
| **1886**<br>28 Oct | | | 1,389 | **E. Harrison** | *Ejecting Cartridges from Breech-loading Firearms* | Abandoned Application Specification not printed |
| **1886**<br>23 Nov | 22 Aug | 27 Sept | 15,272 | **Edgar Harrison**<br>142 New Bond Street | *Improvement in Connection with Hammerless Sporting Breech-loading Firearms*<br><br>Cocking lever (sidelock) | Agent: Brewer & Son<br><br>Illustrated |
| **1886**<br>10 Dec | 1887<br>29 July | 1887<br>23 Sept | 16,214* | **Edgar Harrison**<br>142 New Bond Street | *Improvement in Breech-loading Sporting Firearms* | Agent: Brewer & Son<br><br>Illustrated |
| | | | | Amended, 29 Nov 1888, under Sections 18-21 of the Patents, Designs and Trade Marks Act, 1883. | | |
| **1887**<br>24 Oct | 1888<br>23 July | 1888<br>24 Oct | 14,444 | **Edgar Harrison**<br>142 New Bond Street &<br>**Edwin George Anson**<br>Haydn Villa, Station Rd, Harrow | *An Improved Method of Cocking and Making Safe Hammerless Guns and Rifles*<br><br>Cocking and forend catch | Illustrated |

| | | | | | | |
|---|---|---|---|---|---|---|
| **1888**<br>10 Feb | | | 2,027 | **E. Harrison** &<br>**D. Gibson** | *Cartridge Loading<br>Machines* | Abandoned Application<br>Specification not<br>printed |
| **1888**<br>10 Aug | 1889<br>10 May | 1889<br>22 June | 11,550 | **Edgar Harrison**<br>142 New Bond Street | *Improvement in or<br>Connected with Breech<br>Loading Sporting Firearms*<br><br>*Ejectors* | Agent: Brewer & Son<br>33 Chancery Lane<br><br>Illustrated |
| **1888**<br>12 Dec | 1889<br>12 Sept | 1889<br>19 Oct | 18,157 | **Edgar Harrison**<br>142 New Bond Street | *Improvement in or<br>Connected with Breech<br>Loading Sporting Firearms*<br><br>*Cocking and Ejectors* | Agent: Brewer & Son<br>33 Chancery Lane<br><br>Illustrated |
| **1889**<br>28 Aug | 1890<br>28 May | 1890<br>28 June | 13,591 | **Edgar Harrison**<br>142 New Bond Street | *Improvements in Ejector<br>Mechanism for Breakdown<br>Guns*<br><br>*Ejectors* | Agent: Brewer & Son<br>33 Chancery Lane<br><br>Illustrated |
| **1890**<br>1 May | | | 6,723 | **E. Harrison** | *Stocks for Forearms* | Abandoned Application<br>Specification not printed |
| **1890**<br>11 Dec | 1891<br>10 Oct | 1891<br>14 Nov | 20,234 | **Edgar Harrison**<br>142 New Bond Street | *Improvements in Ejecting<br>Mechanism for Drop Down<br>Sporting Firearms*<br><br>*Ejectors* | Agent: Brewer & Son<br>33 Chancery Lane<br><br>Illustrated |
| **1895**<br>25 Feb | 27 Dec | 1896<br>22 Feb | 4,005 | **Edgar Harrison**<br>29a Gillingham Street | *Improvements in Breech<br>Loading Small Arms*<br><br>*Single trigger mechanism* | Illustrated |
| **1895**<br>1 Mar | | | 4,413 | **E. Harrison** | *Small Arms* | Abandoned Application<br>Specification not printed |
| **1898**<br>22 Jan | | | 1,732 | **E. Harrison** | *Small Arms* | Abandoned Application<br>Specification not printed |
| **1898**<br>19 April | | | 9,009 | **E. Harrison** | *Firearm* | Abandoned Application<br>Specification not printed |
| **1900**<br>3 March | 3 Dec | 1901<br>9 Feb | 4,097 | **Edgar Harrison**<br>29a Gillingham Street | *Improvements in Rifles*<br><br>*Bolt action rifle* | Agents: Newton & Son<br><br>Illustrated |
| **1901**<br>1 July | 1902<br>25 April | 1902<br>5 June | 13,382 | **Edgar Harrison** &<br>**Joseph Vincent Bonel**<br>Both of Small Arms<br>Factory, 9a Gillingham<br>Street, Pimlico | *Improvements relating to<br>Recoil Operated firearms.*<br><br>Locking of bolt in recoil<br>operated firearms | Agents: Newton & Son<br><br>Illustrated |
| **1929**<br>9 May | 1930<br>10 Feb | 1930<br>5 June | 330,105 | **Edgar Harrison**<br>Small Arms Factory,<br>Feltham, Middlesex | *Improvements in Air Pistols* | Agent: Brewer & Son<br>33 Chancery Lane<br>Illustrated |

# Appendix 3: Trade Names and Company Names

## Company Names:

B. Cogswell
E. Harrison & Co. (Cogswell & Harrison)
Cogswell and Harrison Ltd
Cogswell and Harrison (Gunmakers) Ltd
William Moore and William Grey
William Moore and Grey
Wm Moore and Grey

## Trade Names:

| Guns | Cartridges | Gun Powder | Accessories & Products |
|---|---|---|---|
| Ambassardor | Ardit | Cogshultze | Armus (Bicycles) |
| Armus | Avant Tout | Vicmite | Blagdon (Shooting School) |
| Avant Tout | Blagdon | Vicmos | Bulls Eye (Tennis Racket) |
| Blagdon | Blagdonette | | Cogoil (Cleaning Oil) |
| Certus | Bono | | Cogpact (Gun Case) |
| Colonist | Certus | | Cogtite (Boots) |
| Cosmos | Exceltor | | Compactum (Game Carrier) |
| Crown | Farmo | | Coswel (Abrasive Paste) |
| Desideratum | Kelor | | Coswel (Anti-Corrosive Paste) |
| General Purpose | Konkor | | Coswel (Lubricating Fluid) |
| Grand Prix | Konor | | Coswell (Hat) |
| Huntic | Markor | | Dint (Golf Clubs) |
| Konor | Markoroid | | Fusilite (Torch) |
| Longfort | Midget | | Left Eye Master (Corrector) |
| Markor | Molto | | Marvic (Tennis Racket) |
| Modele de Luxe | Pluviod | | Perfecta (Cartridge Bag) |
| Moorgrey | Ranger | | Primic (Binocular) |
| Primic | Swiftsure | | Swiftsure (Clay Trap) |
| Regency | Universal | | Swiftsures (Clay Birds) |
| Rex | Victor | | Twin Definder (Rifle Sight) |
| Rover | Victoriod | | |
| Sandhurst | Victor Universal | | |
| Take Down | Vix | | |
| Tower | Westro | | |
| Twelve Major | | | |
| Twelve Minor | | | |
| Vena Contracta | | | |
| Victor | | | |

# Appendix 4: Cogswell & Harrison Publications

**CATALOGUES:**

| Date | Title | Additional Material |
|------|-------|---------------------|
| 1900 | Cogswell & Harrison | None |
| 1909 | Manufacture d'Armes de Luxe Catalogue in French | None |
| 1912 | Cogswell & Harrison, July 1912 | None |
| 1924 | Sporting Guns Rifles and Accessories | None |
| 1929 | Guns, Rifles & Sporting Equipment, List D 29 | None |
| 1934 | Special List of Best Guns List F 34 | Supplement List G 34 |
| 1946 | A List of Guns and Rifles List D 46 | Covering letter of 7 March 1949 and price list Certus Folding Fourten Gun and Seat Stick insert |
| 1959 | Guns, Rifles, Pistols, Binoculars and Accessories | Price list FT/OT Lyman reloading equipment and price list insert |
| 1964 | Cogswell & Harrison | Price lists November 1964 and February 1965 |
| 1973 | Comprehensive Gun and Accessories Catalogue | Price list 1973 |
| 1978 | General Catalogue Loose Leaf (green cover), July 1978 | None |
| 1978 | General Catalogue Bound (white cover), July 1978 | None |
| 1993 | Cogswell & Harrison Finest Quality Sporting Guns | Price List 1993 to Present |

**BOOKS:**

'Blagdon' (Harrison, Edgar), *Shooting with Game* and *Gun Room Notes,* Cogswell & Harrison, London, 1900
Harrison, Edgar, *A Dissertation upon Guns and Shooting,* Cogswell & Harrison, London, 1906
Harrison, Edgar, *Guns and Shooting,* Cogswell & Harrison, London, 1908
Peskett, John, F., *Bicentenary of a Gunmaker,* Cogswell & Harrison, London, 1969/70
Cogswell & Harrison, *Shooting,* Teach Yourself Books, English Universities Press Ltd, 1970

1900

1912

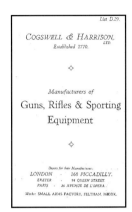

1929

1934

1946

1959

1964

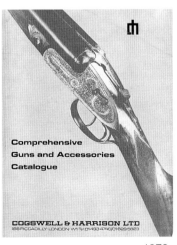

1973

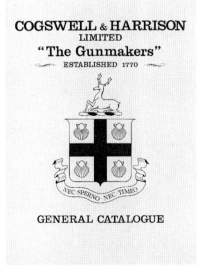

1978

# *Appendix 5: Trade Labels*

1842 - 1863

1893 - 1928

1901 - 1928

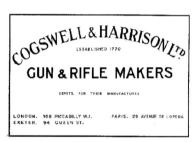

1927 - 1939

1917 - 1930

1927 - 1937

1984 - 1985

1993 to date

The dates given above are only a general guide to the vintage. The labels were multi-address and often continued in use for some years after one of the locations was closed or a new one opened. More precise dates are given in Appendix 1.

# Bibliography

**Books**

Akehurst, R., *Game Guns and Rifles*, The Sportsman's Press, London, 1992.

Beaumont, R., *Purdey's The Guns and the Family,* David & Charles, 1984.

Boothroyd, G., *Gun Collecting*, The Sportsman's Press, London, 1998.

   *Sidelocks and Boxlocks*, Safari Press, California/The Sportsman's Press, London 1998.

Boothroyd, G. & S. Boothroyd, *The British Over-and-Under Shotgun*, The Sportsman's Press, London, 1996.

Brown, N., *London Gunmakers*, Christie's Books, London, 1998.

Burrard, G., *The Modern Shotgun*, Vols I, II, III, Ashford Press Publishing, 1985.

Crudgington, I.M. & D.J. Baker, *The British Shotgun*, Vols I, II, Ashford Buchan & Enright, 1990.

Glendenning, I., *British Pistols and Guns 1640-1840,* Arco Publishing Co. Inc., New York, 1962.

Greener, W.W., *The Gun and its Development*, New Orchard Edition, 1988.

King, P., *The Shooting Field,* Quiller Press, London.

Lancaster, C., *The Art of Shooting*, Charles Lancaster & Co., London, 1942.

Tate, D., *The Birmingham Gun Makers*, Safari Press/The Sportsman's Press, London, 1999.

Teasdale-Buckell, G.T., *Experts on Guns and Shooting*, Ashford Press Publishing, 1986.

Thomas, G., *Gun Book: Shotgun Lore for the Sportsman,* Adam & Charles Black, London, 1977.

   *Shotguns & Cartridges*, Adam & Charles Black, London, 1981.


**Journals**

Anon., 'A Gun for each Century', *The Field* 23 July 1970, p 190.

Aronsson, A.' 'Exklusiv Bössmakare Kommer Tillbaka', *Jaktmarker & Fiskevatten*, No.11, 1994, pp 58/59.

Bell, S., 'British Doubles from A-Z', Part ix, *Double Gun Journal*, Vol 10, Issue 3, Autumn 1999, pp 26-27.

Boothroyd, G., 'The Avant Tout Hammergun', *Shooting Times*, 31 January 1991, p 37.

   'Taking Stock', *Shooting Times*, 21-27 October 1995.

   'Cogswell & Harrison Ltd London', *Double Gun Journal*, Vol iii, Issue 3, Autumn 1997, pp 101-106.

   Grant, D., 'Aiming for the Top', *Shooting Times* , Issue 4916, 11 July 1997, pp 32-33.

   'For Princes and Poachers: England's oldest gunmaker is reborn…', *The Shooting Gazette*, April 1996, pp 26-28.

Jackson, T., 'Cogswell & Harrison: Like a Phoenix from the Ashes…', *Shooting Sportsman*, Vol viii, Issue 1, Jan/Feb 1996, pp 42-45.

   'Cogswell & Harrison: The Old and the New', *Magnum*, Vol 22, No. 11, November 1997, pp 20-22.

Newton, J., 'An Odd Ball Gun; The Cogswell and Harrison Cosmos Ball and Shot Gun', *Guns Review*, Vol 36, No. 10, Oct 1996, pp 745-747.

   'The Origins of Clay Pigeon Shooting', *The Gun Collector*, Vol 1, Issue 2, Summer 1997, pp 28-31.

   'Eye for an Eye', *Shooting Times and Country Magazine*, 16 October 1997, pp 51-53.

   'Vital Cog in Action', *Shooting Times*, 21 October 1999, pp 34-36.

Sundseth, D., 'To Klassiske Sideliggere: Cogswell & Harrison', *Våpenjournalen*, No. 2, 1995, pp 28-31.

# Index